YOU ARE ONE OF THE SELECT FEW
CHOSEN TO PARTICIPATE IN
THIS MAGNIFICENT ENTERPRISE.
YOU ARE A LUNAR PIONEER

*WELCOME TO MOONBASE*
A NEW WORLD. A NEW WAY OF LIFE.

Welcome to the exciting, dynamic, growing community that is humankind's first permanent settlement beyond the planet Earth. That you have accepted the unique opportunity and challenge to join us at Moonbase is proof of your pioneer spirit, special skills, and burning curiosity—the qualities which will help our settlement grow and prosper. *Welcome to Moonbase* will serve as your introduction and guide to an extraordinary island of culture, science, and industry in space.

Inside, you'll find everything you want to know about Moonbase: its history and its future, its quality of life and work, its intriguing scientific advances in research and exploration. You are ready to embark on a remarkable journey into a world of infinite possibilities. Share in the grand design of our proud human endeavor; discover the beauty and desolation of the lunar landscape. Welcome aboard! Your adventure is about to begin.

MOONBASE.
IT'S LIKE NO PLACE
YOU'VE EVER BEEN BEFORE.

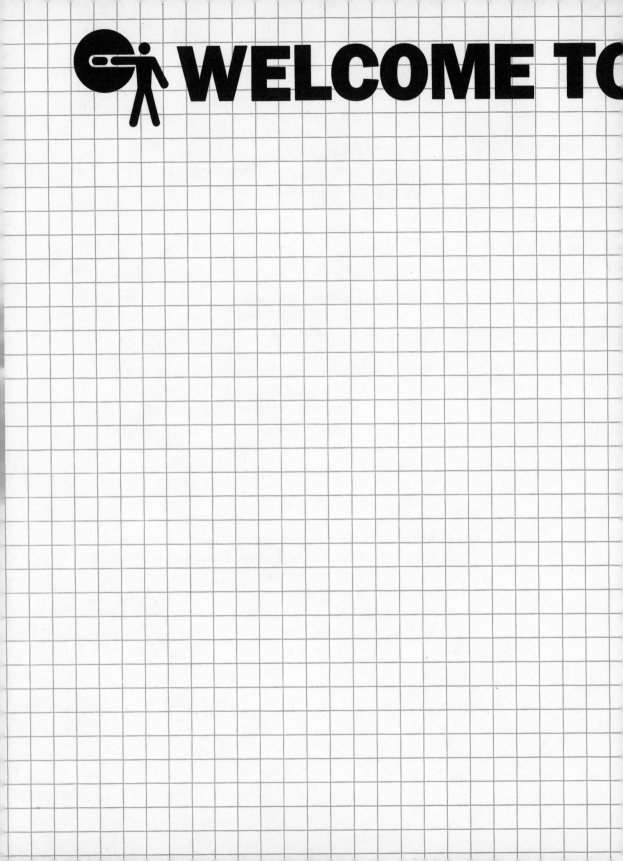

# WELCOME TO

# MOONBASE

## BEN BOVA

ILLUSTRATIONS BY PAT RAWLINGS

BALLANTINE BOOKS · NEW YORK

Copyright © 1987 by Ben Bova
Illustrations copyright © 1987 by R. Patrick Rawlings

All rights reserved under International and Pan-American Copyright
Conventions. Published in the United States by Ballantine Books,
a division of Random House, Inc., New York, and simultaneously
in Canada by Random House of Canada Limited, Toronto.

Library of Congress Catalog Card Number: 86-92093

ISBN: 0-345-32859-0

Cover design by Dale Fiorillo
Cover illustration by R. Patrick Rawlings
Text design by Alex Jay/Studio J

Manufactured in the United States of America

First Edition: November 1987

10 9 8 7 6 5 4 3 2 1

To all the men and women
who are making our return
to the Moon possible,
but especially to Hu Davis.

# Contents

**Foreword**

Welcome to Moonbase!

Welcome to the exciting, dynamic, growing community that is humankind's first permanent settlement beyond the planet Earth. We need outstanding men and women here on this new frontier, and we are delighted that you have decided to work and live with us on the Moon.

By choosing to spend a year at Moonbase you have shown that you have the pioneer spirit, the skills, and the dedication we need to help our settlement grow and prosper. The work you have come here to do will be exciting, challenging, and extremely important. The screening procedures and tests that you have passed prove that you are the kind of person who can be a positive asset to our growing community.

This manual will tell you what you need to know to orient yourself in Moonbase. It will help you to learn who we are, how we operate, and what we do for our people. You will see that we are a socially responsible organization, dedicated to quality and excellence in everything we do—and that includes our relationship with you.

There are many advantages to working at Moonbase. These include high pay, a wide range of benefits, the best working conditions in the solar system, and promising career opportunities.

Life on the Moon can be very different from life on Earth or aboard a space station. You will spend your first week at Moonbase getting acquainted with your neighbors and coworkers, and with the job you have come here to do. You will also be getting acquainted with living mostly underground, in low gravity.

The people you meet and work with are people very much like you. Although they come from all walks of life, from many different nations and races, they are all highly skilled, highly motivated, and dedicated to making their year at Moonbase productive and rewarding.

Many of them have already decided to extend their work contracts beyond the one-year minimum. Some have decided to live at Moonbase permanently. Perhaps you will, too.

Whether you leave us after one year or extend your stay and eventually become a Moonbase citizen, we want to welcome you aboard. We think you will find Moonbase an excellent place to live and work. We wish you a successful and happy stay on the Moon.

Sincerely,
*Human Resources Division*
*Moonbase, Inc.*

**Introduction:
A Walk
on the Moon**

"Magnificent desolation," was astronaut Edwin (Buzz) Aldrin's description of the Moon as he and Neil Armstrong planted the first human footprints on the dusty lunar surface.

The Moon is rugged, barren, desolate—and magnificent. One of the first things that every newcomer to Moonbase wants to do is to pull on a space suit, dog down the helmet, and take a walk on the surface of this new world.

The first thing you notice about the Moon is that the horizon seems strangely close. And, unlike the gentle vistas of Earth, the lunar horizon is a sharp line that abruptly divides the solid rocky world from the utterly black depths of space.

The horizon *is* close: because the Moon is only about one-quarter the size of Earth, the horizon is only about half the distance it would be on Earth. And it is sharp; on the airless Moon there is no atmospheric haze to soften the distant views.

A harsh, unforgiving world, it seems at first. A world without air, without water, where the days last 350 hours and the noontime temperature can reach 134° Celsius (273° Fahrenheit), higher than the boiling point of water. The "overnight lows" can go down to −153° C (−243° F). The Moon is utterly lifeless—except for the life we from Earth have brought to it.

Yet there is beauty on the Moon.

Although the sun sets for some 350 hours at Moonbase's latitude, there is seldom any true "night" on the lunar surface. This is because the Earth is always hanging in the lunar sky, shining up to fifty times brighter than the full Moon on

Earth, so bright that you can read even the fine print of a contract with ease.

It is a breathtakingly beautiful sight, the blue and white orb of Earth; a sight that is always present in the skies above Moonbase, every day, every night, all year long. Even during the "new Earth" phase, when we see only the night side of our home world, it is ringed with a glorious blue halo of light refracted by the atmosphere, and the innumerable lights of cities dot its darkened face.

The lunar surface is barren, truly. Not a blade of grass or a drop of water. Nothing but rocks and craters, from tiny pebbles to boulders the size of apartment buildings, from fingertip-sized holes in the ground to mammoth ringwalls hundreds of miles across. And mountains that soar miles high.

But look again. Despite its forbidding appearance, the lunar landscape is far gentler than you might expect. For billions of years this rocky surface has been sandpapered by a constant infall of tiny bits of meteoric dust that have smoothed every boulder and mountain peak. Larger meteoroid strikes have blasted out craters. Subsurface "volcanism," mere seepages of thin gases rather than explosive terrestrial-type volcanoes, have caused some parts of the surface to slump and collapse into sinuous rilles and potholes.

When you step out across the lunar soil your boots stir up clouds of dust that spread and fall slowly, lazily back to the ground. The Moon is a slow-motion world, with a gravity pull only one-sixth that of Earth. If you trip and fall, you can put out a hand, push, and spring back to your feet easily. There is plenty of time to do so.

While the surface soil is dark, you notice that the footprints you leave behind you are much brighter. The lighter color is the true tone of the soil; the surface has been darkened by eons of hard radiation from the Sun. Such radiation never reaches the Earth's surface; the terrestrial atmosphere absorbs it. On the Moon, your space suit—referred to by Moonbasers as a "hard suit"—provides radiation protection.

Dawn on the Moon is breathtaking. Without air to diffuse the Sun's light, the difference between night and day is virtually instantaneous. One moment you are in darkness, the next in full brilliant sunlight. Because the Moon rotates so slowly, you can keep pace with the day–night terminator line by walking!

The dark sky does not fade with sunrise. The stars still hang above, without twinkling. You can watch the line of daylight touch the distant mountain peaks and work its way down toward you until you are bathed in brightness and the ground around you lights up.

At some locations near Moonbase the ground literally sparkles at sunrise, as if millions of jewels were sprinkled across the landscape. The phosphorescent effect is the result of minerals in the soil reacting to the sudden heat and light energy from the Sun.

Moonwalks can be exhilarating. Especially the first time, when the unique beauties of the Moon are brand-new experiences. While the first impression a

LUNAR PHASES: TOP VIEW

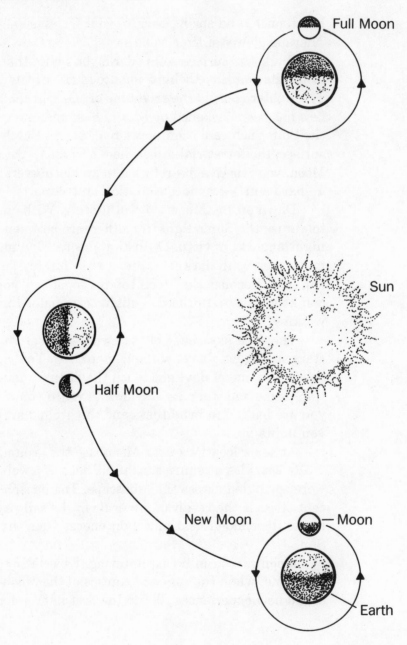

Full Moon

Sun

Half Moon

New Moon

Moon

Earth

newcomer gets when looking at the lunar surface is one of emptiness and desolation, gradually you begin to appreciate the true beauty of the Moon. The silence, the dramatic vistas, the rugged grandeur, the complete *otherworldliness* of the Moon slowly overtakes you. Walking on the surface has become one of the principal recreations of Moonbase's inhabitants and visitors. And making footprints in the lunar soil, literally "where no man has gone before," is a once-in-a-lifetime thrill.

---

### ONE DAY PER MONTH

To this day, some people still believe there is a "dark side" of the Moon.

The Moon rotates. Its "day" is 27 Earth days, 7 hours, 27 minutes long. That is the same period as its orbit around the Earth, so that a lunar "day" is exactly the same length as a month.

Astronomers say that the Moon's rotation is "locked," so that it always keeps one side facing the Earth. The other side is never seen from Earth. Both sides, however, receive the same amount of sunlight; each side of the Moon is in daylight approximately fourteen Earth days, and in darkness for the same length of time. There is no "dark side" of the Moon.

At Moonbase, the Earth-facing side of the Moon is usually called the near side or the Earth side. The side that never sees Earth is called, prosaically, the far side.

---

**How to Use
This Manual**

The Moonbase orientation manual is designed for easy use by the reader. Each section is clearly marked and written so as to be understandable independently of all other sections. Therefore it is possible to read the specific sections that interest you most without needing to read the sections that precede it.

For example, if you are primarily interested in living conditions at Moonbase, you may turn to the section titled "Quality of Life" immediately. There is no need to read the preceding sections first.

However, the Manual is arranged in a logical order, presenting the history of Moonbase, living conditions, descriptions of the major lunar industries, and a view of Moonbase's future—in that order. The physical facts of the lunar environment are given in Appendix 1.

# Welcome
# to Moonbase

# Our Proud Heritage: Moonbase History

"Houston, Tranquility Base here. The Eagle has landed."

These were the first words said on the Moon, spoken by Neil Armstrong. The date was 20 July 1969. Billions of people around the Earth watched Armstrong take the first steps onto the dusty lunar surface. Yet by the end of 1972 the Apollo program had been terminated, and no one set foot on the Moon again until 17 August 1999, when Vladimir Borkovsky led the first Russian lunar landing mission.

## The Years Between

Why the twenty-seven-year hiatus between human visits to the Moon?

The original Apollo program was launched mainly for political reasons. The Americans perceived themselves to be in a race against Soviet Russia, and mounted a massive $24 billion effort to be the first to reach the Moon. They succeeded so well that by the time of their final mission, Apollo 17, flights to the Moon were accepted as routine by most of the world's media and public. Except for the ill-fated Apollo 13, which suffered nearly catastrophic damage on its way to the Moon, all the Apollo missions went quite smoothly. And the three astronauts of Apollo 13 were returned to Earth safe and unharmed, in a display of technical brilliance and innovative daring that is still hardly equaled in the annals of space flight.

The Apollo program did not lead to continuous human occupation of the Moon for two reasons.

First, because the program's main goal was to

reach the Moon as quickly as possible, the Apollo missions were designed to go directly from Earth to lunar orbit. Once in orbit around the Moon, two Apollo astronauts detached their landing vehicle from the main spacecraft and descended to the lunar surface for times varying from slightly more than 21 hours (Apollo 11) to just under 75 hours (Apollo 17). In all, twelve astronauts spent a total of 300 hours, 1 minute, and 29 seconds on the surface of the Moon.

Although the astronauts conducted some rudimentary geological studies, brought back a total of 384.2 kilograms (845.2 pounds) of lunar rocks for more detailed examination by scientists, and left arrays of scientific instruments on the Moon for further observations, the Apollo program was a dead end, scientifically, technically, and politically. No hardware remained in space that could be used again. No space station had been built in Earth orbit, where it might have been used for other purposes. Even the instruments left functioning on the lunar surface were turned off by 1977, in a move by the American government to save money.

Second, each Apollo mission cost on the order of $500 million. Using the huge Saturn V booster and a spacecraft that had to land by parachute at sea (which necessitated a considerable fleet of ships to find and recover the astronauts and their return module) meant that the Apollo missions were too costly to be continued. To spend $24 billion for a total of some twelve and a half days on the Moon was hardly cost-efficient!

The first Soviet missions to the Moon benefited from the American experience. After their daring attempt to land the first human explorers on the surface of the planet Mars in 1992, the Soviet Union began an ambitious series of lunar landings that included stays on the lunar surface of up to two weeks at a time by teams of six cosmonauts and scientists.

But even though the Americans had not aimed for the Moon since 1972, the U.S. space program was moving inexorably toward a return there.

In 1981 the first flight of the U.S. space shuttle opened the door to a new era of space operations. The shuttle was almost completely reusable, and lowered the cost of going into low Earth orbit (LEO). Since it takes much more energy to go from the Earth's surface to LEO than it does to go from LEO to a soft lunar landing, the shuttle was a vital first step toward the return to the Moon.

Even after the disastrous loss of seven astronauts in the *Challenger* accident of 1986, the U.S. utilized improved versions of the shuttle and, later, the all-reusable spaceplane as the backbone of its space endeavors.

**The Space Stations**

Since 1971 the Soviet Union had orbited a series of Salyut space stations, most of which were occupied by teams of two or three cosmonauts at a time. The first seven Salyuts were eventually deorbited and dropped into the deep ocean, after which a new space station was launched. Their eighth station, Mir, became the first permanent space station, with new modules added to it from time to time.

In 1973 the Americans had established a temporary space station, Skylab, constructed from modules left over from the aborted Apollo program. Plagued with technical difficulties from its start, occupied by only three teams of astronauts, and abandoned after early 1974, the empty Skylab plunged back to Earth in a spectacular reentry in 1979. Most of it fell harmlessly into the Indian Ocean, although a few fragments reached the ground in western Australia.

In 1998 the U.S. completed construction of its first permanent space station. By far the largest structure to be built in LEO up to that time, it was joined by a Western European station, Columbus, and several other segments build by private industrial companies. The U.S. space station, in addition to becoming a nexus for scientific, commercial, and industrial operations in orbit, was the first real step toward the American return to the Moon.

**LEGEND**
LAUNCH VEHICLES
A. 1998 Unmanned heavy-lift launch vehicle
B. 2001 National Aerospace plane/ transatmospheric vehicle
C. 2010 Reuseable heavy-lift launch vehicle
HISTORICAL LAUNCH VEHICLES
D. Late-1960s Saturn rocket
E. 1980s shuttle

ORBITAL AND EXTRAORBITAL VEHICLES
F. 1994 Orbital Transfer Vehicle
G. 1996 Aerobraking OTV
H. 2015 Lunar shuttle
I. 2020 Nuclear electrical power space freighter
  1. 5 Mw space nuclear reactor

J. 2010 Hybrid zero-G/ variable g space station
  1. Multi-story habitation module
  2. Winches
  3. Hi-strength Kevlar cables
  4. Zero-G area
  5. Dynamic solar collectors
  6. Space nuclear reactor
  7. Pressurized hangar
  8. Astromast
  9. Trolley

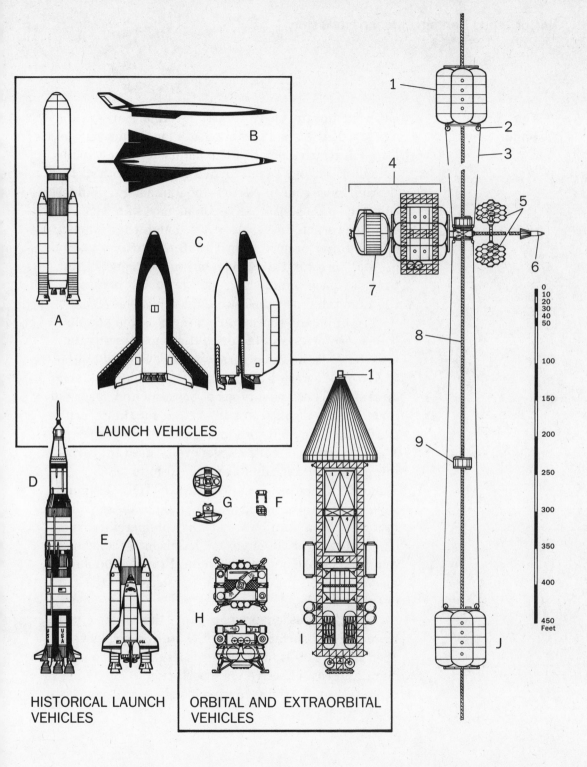

LAUNCH VEHICLES

A

B

C

HISTORICAL LAUNCH
VEHICLES

D

E

ORBITAL AND EXTRAORBITAL
VEHICLES

F

G

H

I

1

1

2

3

4

5

6

7

8

9

J

0
10
20
30
40
50

100

150

200

250

300

350

400

450
Feet

9

**The "Lunar Underground"**

Even during the early 1980s, the American space agency, NASA, had established a small but energetic Lunar Initiative office at the Johnson Space Center, outside Houston, Texas. In Washington, both at the White House and in NASA's headquarters, planners saw the space station program as part of a concerted effort to return to the Moon. Although there was no official lunar program until 1995, a "lunar underground" grew within the government agencies and the aerospace community, quietly laying plans for the inevitable permanent occupancy of the Moon.

To build the space station in LEO and supply the laboratories and factories that were springing up around it, new spacecraft were developed by the U.S., the Western Europeans, the Russians, and the Japanese. These new types of boosters and space vehicles would also become important for the return to the Moon. They fell into four general categories:

1. Improved shuttles, generally used for carrying personnel and high-priority cargo to LEO. Among the first of these was the HOTOL, designed in Great Britain, which was capable of taking off and landing like a jet airliner at any commercial airport. (HOTOL was an acronym for HOrizontal TakeOff and Landing.) The Soviet Union, France, and Japan also developed shuttle vehicles of various sizes and capabilities.

The 235-passenger spaceplane that carried you from Earth's surface to an LEO station was developed in the 1990s for two purposes: to provide efficient and cost-effective transportation to LEO, and to provide equally swift and inexpensive transportation from point to point on Earth—such as the two-hour flight from New York to Beijing.

2. Heavy lift vehicles, for carrying bulk payloads of 300 tons or more to LEO. Often referred to as "big dumb boosters," these unmanned craft are still our primary freight carriers, lifting heavy cargo from the Earth's surface. Often their empty rocket stages are dismantled in orbit and used for new structural material, while their engines and guidance systems are returned to Earth by high-capacity shuttles.

3. Orbital Maneuvering Vehicles (OMVs), small, mostly unmanned craft based at a space station and used to deploy other satellites from the station and/ or bring malfunctioning satellites to the space station for maintenance and repair. The backpack Manned Maneuvering Units (MMU) used by individual astronauts are, in a sense, the smallest OMVs.

4. Orbital Transfer Vehicle (OTVs), spacecraft that are assembled in orbit and intended to remain in space rather than return to Earth. These are used to move personnel and materials from one orbit to another. For example, OTVs carry people and equipment from the space stations at LEO up to the stations in geosynchronous Earth orbit (GEO), where communications satellites hover in stationary 24-hour orbits.

The OTVs developed for the space station program had the inherent capability of going from LEO to lunar orbit (the energy required is no more than that needed to attain GEO); all they needed to deliver heavy cargos to lunar orbit were additional strap-on propellant tanks for their rocket engines. By the time the Russians made their first landing on the Moon, the Americans had most of the hardware necessary to go from their space station to orbits close to the lunar surface. Indeed, when they returned to the Moon two years after the first Soviet landing, they used modified OTVs for the flight from LEO to lunar orbit, and other modified OTVs for the actual landings on the surface.

One additional capability was brought to fruition during the development of the space station: robotics. The original U.S. space station was designed to be highly automated. Many of its systems were operated by sophisticated computers programmed to run semi-independently of human control—with the so-called Artificial Intelligence (AI) programs. The space station also included an array of teleoperated systems, in which a human operator inside the station remotely controlled equipment outside the station. AI, teleoperation, and other advances in computer hardware and software led to the robotic systems that are used so heavily throughout Moonbase.

**The Return to the Moon**

On 8 November 2001 astronaut Shiela Davidson, in command of a six-person team of astronauts and scientists, landed her Diana spacecraft (a modified OTV) on the surface of the Ocean of Storms, within sight of the dormant hardware left there by the Apollo 12 astronauts nearly thirty-two years earlier.

Davidson's first words upon setting foot on the Moon proved to be prophetic:

"We're back, and this time we're here to stay!"

The Americans were indeed back on the Moon. But they were no longer alone there. An all-male Soviet team of six was exploring the Sea of Crises, more than a thousand kilometers east-northeast of the Diana 1 landing site. Nor was the crew of Diana 1 entirely American. Among the four scientists were a British geologist, a West German geochemist, and a French-Canadian astronomer.

The Americans were back on the Moon to stay— with their Atlantic Community allies—because by the year 2001 there were solid economic reasons for returning to the Moon.

First, the costs of reaching the Moon had come down several orders of magnitude from the old days of Apollo. With spaceplanes to reach LEO, space stations to serve as staging areas and efficient OTV-like spacecraft, sending teams to the Moon was little more costly than lifting them from Earth's surface to a space station in LEO.

Second, building space stations had led to the development of long-term life support systems and extensive experience in living and working in space, under zero-gravity conditions. Also, computer systems and robotics had advanced significantly during the final two decades of the twentieth century. This meant that the men and women heading for the Moon need not spend years in specialized training. The spacecraft and support systems were so highly automated and reliable that scientists and engineers could travel to the Moon as passengers; they needed no more flight training than they needed to fly in the spaceplanes of the 1990s.

Finally, the expansion of industrial and commercial operations in LEO dictated a return to the Moon so that lunar resources could be used as raw materials for the construction and manufacturing activities underway at LEO.

Studies of the lunar rocks and soil samples brought to Earth by the Apollo astronauts had shown that the Moon's surface is rich in aluminum, silicon, oxygen, titanium, magnesium, and even iron. All of these elements were important raw materials for the factories and other facilities that were being built in LEO.

Because the Moon's gravitational pull is only one-sixth that of Earth, and because the Moon has no atmosphere, it takes very little energy to boost a payload from the lunar surface. In fact, it is twenty-two times less expensive (in terms of energy) to lift a pound from the moon and bring it to LEO than it is to lift a pound from the Earth to LEO—even though the low Earth orbit in question may be only a hundred miles from Earth's surface!

With private industrial corporations manufacturing pharmaceuticals, plastics, crystals, new metal alloys, and electronic materials in LEO, with the Japanese constructing the first Solar Power Satellites, with the possibility of military satellites requiring heavy tonnages of shielding material, the potential of lunar raw materials became an economic driving force.

Moonbase's first "export" product was oxygen derived from the regolith. Construction materials and raw materials for orbital factories followed soon afterward.

**The Heroic Years**

Like Rome, Moonbase was not built in a day.

The first few years after the Diana 1 landing of 2001 saw a continuing stream of men and women exploring the Moon and learning how to live and work there.

Those were the years for heroes and heroines. Living in prefabricated shelters dug into shallow trenches and covered with lunar rubble, working in cumbersome pressurized suits, being exposed to the dangers of radiation and the unknown with no back-up closer than a quarter-million miles away, these scientist/explorers paved the way for the permanent occupation of the Moon.

Their names are legend.

Every schoolchild knows of Mason, Lenoire, and Wayne, who made the first overland traverse on the Moon in 2006. Their 2,500-kilometer (more than 1,550-mile) route took them around the rim of Mare Imbrium from the crater Copernicus to Eratosthenes, along the north face of the Apennine Mountains and over to the Apollo 15 landing site at Hadley Rille, then across the crater Archimedes to the walled plain Plato, finally ending at Sinus Iridium.

DelCorso led the twelve-person trek across the Oceanus Procellarum in 2008, starting at the crater Aristarchus and penetrating into the Mare Nubium as far as the crater Opelt before running so short of supplies that his team had to be rescued.

The Soviet expedition of 2009 completed the first successful circumnavigation of the Moon, although the team did not travel overland but used a ballistic rocket vehicle to "hop" from one preselected landing site to another. Fresh propellants and supplies were waiting for them at each landing site. The Soviet expedition, led by F. A. Korolev, was the first to make geological studies of the lunar far side and to return rock samples to Earth from that side of the Moon which never faces Earth.

These and many other daring and dangerous explorations of the lunar surface had many different goals and purposes, but one overriding aim attended them all: the search for water.

Since the earliest studies of the lunar rocks brought to Earth by the Apollo astronauts, no trace of water had been found on the Moon. The rock and soil samples were completely anhydrous: there was no water in them, not even chemically bound to other elements.

Galileo thought that the large dark areas of the lunar surface might actually be bodies of water when he first observed the Moon with a telescope in 1609. But four centuries of observation showed conclusively that liquid water could not exist on the Moon's surface, and the lunar "maria" are not seas but vast stretches of dark rock. Although liquid water seemed out of the question, some astronomers theorized that ice might lie frozen beneath the lunar surface, or in permanently shadowed "cold traps" inside certain craters or at the Moon's poles.

The ill-fated Brennart expedition of 2012 set out specifically to search for ice pockets in the north polar region. When the nine-person team was caught in a radiation storm following a large solar flare, they were able to reach the relative safety of a natural cave in the lee of a crater wall. Their communications and other electronics equipment, however, were severely damaged by the high radiation flux. Unable to operate their crawlers, and unable to radio for help, they were rescued by a relief mission only after five of the explorers had died of oxygen starvation.

The Brennart expedition did not find ice at the lunar north pole. Nor has any explorer yet found water in any form during all the years of searching. Still the search continues.

LUNAR LEGENDS:
THE BRENNART RESCUE

The nine-man Brennart expedition of 2012 was caught in a major solar radiation storm while searching for pockets of ice in permanently shadowed craters near the lunar north pole.

With only a six-hour warning of the impending radiation cloud, Brennart and his all-male team sought safety in a cave in the side of the crater Nansen F, part of a complex of craters named after the Norwegian Arctic explorer Fridtjof Nansen.

The intense radiation flux destroyed most of the electrical equipment aboard Brennart's ground vehicles, including the drive motors and the communications gear. For eight days the men languished in the cave, thousands of kilometers from the nearest lunar base, unable to communicate with the outside world.

"They'll find us," Brennart reassured his men, time and again. "It's only a matter of time. They're searching for us right now."

He was entirely right. A massive search and rescue operation was underway, stretching from space stations in orbit near the Earth to volunteers flying makeshift scouting rockets around the polar region. One of those scouts spotted the abandoned ground vehicles and directed the rescue teams to Nansen F.

Four of the trapped men had already died from oxygen starvation when the rescue team finally made radio contact with the survivors. A fifth died before the rescuers could reach them: Albert J. Brennart himself, who had unselfishly refused to share in the last oxygen bottle left to the remaining men, knowing that it would not be enough to sustain five men until the rescuers arrived with fresh supplies.

His last words were, "I told you they'd find us. I knew they wouldn't let us down."

The explorers are not all human beings. During the latter 1990s and throughout the years of the twenty-first century, satellites have girdled the Moon, constantly mapping, scanning with remote sensors for natural resources, and serving as communications relays from point to point along the lunar surface.

Automated exploration vehicles have traversed every major mare, and today teleoperated vehicles work on the lunar surface constantly, guided by human directors safe in their underground control centers at Moonbase.

**The First Bases**

By 2009, several temporary bases had been established on the Moon. The Soviet Union set up a ring of twelve-person shelters along the southern perimeter of Mare Imbrium, very close to the route of the original Mason, Lenoire, and Wayne traverse. Two years later the Russians built a larger base capable of housing two dozen people inside the crater Aristarchus, on the western edge of Imbrium.

Meanwhile, the United States concentrated its efforts in the Mare Nubium region, setting up three small bases there and linking them with automated surface rovers. The Western European nations established a nine-person base in the highlands near the crater Hipparchus, while a joint Sino-Japanese base, big enough for three dozen people, was placed in the northeast quadrant of Mare Vaporum.

Living conditions in these temporary shelters were primitive, compared to the modern Moonbase. The shelters were designed only for temporary occupancy, and were frequently left unattended, except for automated machinery.

The American shelters, for example, could house up to twelve people but were actually occupied by no more than six at a time, except in emergencies. The teams using these shelters consisted mainly of:

Geologists* who studied the structure of the lunar surface formations and subsurface rock.

Seismologists who probed the Moon's interior to understand its structure and dynamics.

Geochemists who analyzed the composition of the lunar rocks, soil, subsurface. Together with the geologists and seismologists they made many traverses, seeking the richest sites of aluminum, titanium, and other valuable resources. (Silicon and oxygen are abundant virtually everywhere.) Among the important discoveries they made were deposits of gallium, which is used in manufacturing electronics; valuable sources of sulfur, ammonia, and methane; and lodes of high-grade nickel-steel found in large metallic meteorites.

Physicists who studied the interaction of the solar wind with the Moon's surface, particularly the electrical effects.

Astronomers and astrophysicists who studied the Sun, the Earth's geomagnetic field, and the solar wind.

Medical doctors and psychologists who looked after the physical and emotional health of the explorers and studied the effects of low gravity on the human body and isolation on the human mind.

Engineers who began to develop low-gravity construction techniques using native lunar materials as well as prefabricated structures brought from Earth. They also tested techniques developed on Earth to

---

*The word *geology* comes from the study of the Earth (*geo* being the Greek root for *earth*), but is used now for geological studies of any solid planetary body. *Selenology* is specifically the study of the Moon as an astronomical body.

extract oxygen from the topmost layer of the lunar soil, called the regolith.

The temporary shelters were "temporary" only in the sense that no single person lived in one of them for more than three months at a time. Individuals and crews were rotated back to Earth regularly, but the shelters remained in service for many years. Some of them are still in use, with modernized life support systems.

You can visit two of these early shelters which have been preserved in their original condition for tourists. One of them is on the floor of the crater Alphonsus, within easy walking distance of Moonbase. The other is on Mare Nubium. (See the "Footprints in Moondust" section, p. 188)

The shelters resembled segments of the space stations that orbited near the Earth. They were essentially metal canisters, placed in shallow trenches dug out of the lunar regolith by teleoperated crawlers controlled from lunar-orbiting satellites, and then covered with rocky rubble to insulate them and shield their interiors from solar and cosmic radiation.

Each shelter contained living accommodations, life support systems, and the necessary equipment for its crew. In no sense were any of the life support systems completely closed-cycle: water, food, and oxygen had to be supplied biweekly, and often more frequently. Electrical power was provided originally by small nuclear generators, and later by solarvoltaic cells manufactured on the Moon from lunar silicon.

Surface transportation consisted of electrically driven crawlers, descendants of the Lunar Roving Vehicles of the Apollo program of the 1960s.

LUNAR LEGENDS:
THE TRAVELING STILL

During the "heroic" years, when small teams of explorers lived in temporary shelters for a few months at a time, a persistent rumor arose concerning an alcohol-producing still. Although no one admits to actually seeing the apparatus, or partaking of its product, almost everyone who worked on the Moon at that time insisted that they knew someone who had.

According to the tales, the still had originally been made by a NASA astronaut (always unnamed), and it was small enough to be disassembled and moved quickly from one location to another. In various versions of the story the still used yeast, frozen fruits from ration kits, rubbing alcohol, and even rocket propellants as ingredients. The output, known as "rocket juice" or "Moon booze," was alleged to be powerful enough to melt the regolith down to a depth of one full meter.

Even when Moonbase was formally organized, the legend of the still was very much alive. One of the first Moonbase administrators, asked if the legend were true, replied, "Well, you've got a bunch of very bright, very inventive people up here. Either they actually have built the damned thing or they've concocted a great story about it!"

Life at a "tempo," as the early shelters were often called, was difficult at best. Lack of living space, lack of privacy, scarcity of water for washing, monotonous food, and continuous danger combined to strain the nerves of even the hardiest and most stable personalities. Several Americans likened the conditions to those aboard a nuclear submarine, or at a base in Antarctica. Physical endurance and emotional balance were vitally important.

Those early explorers had one advantage, however, over submariners and Antarctic researchers. They could walk out on the lunar surface—albeit within the confines of a cumbersome pressurized space suit (the type now called a "hard suit"). The magnificent vistas of the lunar landscape, and the endlessly beautiful orb of Earth hanging in the blackness of space, provided a spiritual outlet that could not be found anywhere on Earth.

Psychologists quickly found that the low lunar gravity was a positive benefit to the explorers' sense of well-being. Magnifying their muscular strength by a factor of six, these early lunar inhabitants found that they enjoyed working—and playing—in low *g*.

To support these surface shelters and the teams using them, an infrastructure had to be established in space. Just as a team climbing Mt. Everest must have supporting groups that extend from their home nations to the base of the mountain itself and even its lower slopes, the teams exploring the Moon in those pioneering days needed supporting groups that extended from the surface of the Earth to space stations orbiting the Moon itself.

The major resupply centers were in space stations orbiting Earth. From them, supplies and replacement personnel could be sent to the Moon on minimum-energy trajectories that took approximately three days to go from LEO to lunar orbit. In emergencies, high-thrust trajectories could cover the same distance in twenty-four hours or less.

The United States and the Soviet Union both established space stations in "halo" orbits at the L1 libration point above the Moon's near side. (See box on libration points.) The U.S. station was shared with the Western European and Sino-Japanese lunar explorers. From these two stations, equipment, supplies, and personnel could be sent to a surface base within a matter of hours after being requested. In an important demonstration of the East–West cooperation that has characterized the development of the Moon, the United States and the Soviet Union agreed to open their lunar space stations to each other.

Such cooperation had long been a fact on the Moon's surface. Men and women living under difficult, lonely, and often dangerous conditions tend to ignore political ideology and work together. Whenever an individual or a team was in trouble, the people nearest to the problem sent help, regardless of nationality. And long before such activities were officially sanctioned by their governments on Earth, lunar explorers conducted social visits, shared equipment and supplies, and even exchanged teams from one base to another to conduct joint scientific studies and explorations. Especially on holidays such as Christmas, Tet, and May Day, teams on the surface of the Moon somehow managed to get together for impromptu celebrations.

## THE FIRST CHRISTMAS ON THE MOON

December 2003 saw the first celebration of Christmas on the Moon. The six occupants of Tempo D, a lunar shelter situated on the eastern edge of Mare Nubium, within sight of the crater Alphonsus, began decorating their austere underground shelter several days before Christmas with colored ribbons, draw ings, and even a Christmas tree—made of aluminum strips cut from discarded food wrappings, fastened to the stump of an antenna from a nonfunctioning radio.

To their surprise, the six men and women of Tempo D were joined the day before Christmas by two men and a woman from Tempo A, who had scaled the Alphonsus ringwall mountains to join the celebration.

On Christmas day itself, four Russians arrived in a ground vehicle, having traveled overland from their shelter several hundred kilometers to the north.

Christmas dinner consisted of prepackaged frozen turkey, Beluga caviar, and plum pudding that was liberally laced with brandy—apparently brought to the feast by a British physicist who was part of the Tempo A contingent.

Each shelter or temporary base also kept at least one launch vehicle on hand, in case an emergency forced the crew to leave the shelter. These

launch vehicles were capable of reaching a rendezvous with the lunar space stations.

---

### EARTH–MOON LIBRATION POINTS

There are five libration points in space
around the Earth–Moon system. They are
called *Lagrangian* points, after the French
astronomer-mathematician Joseph Louis
Lagrange (1736–1813) who first showed
that libration points exist.

The L1 point is approximately 58,000 kilometers (36,000 miles) above the Moon's near
side. L2 is a slightly farther distance above
the far side. L3 is a point on the Moon's orbit
precisely on the opposite side of Earth. The
L4 and L5 positions are also on the Moon's orbit, equidistant from Earth and Moon. They
are the locations where large permanent
space colonies may one day be constructed.

While objects placed at L4 and L5 will
remain in those locations, drifting back and
forth only slightly as they orbit sixty degrees
ahead of and behind the Moon, the other libration points are not stable positions. Objects
placed there will be ejected into trajectories
that will eventually impact the Earth or the
Moon.

The lunar space station at L1, therefore,
uses rocket thrusters to keep itself in place.
It wanders in a circular halo orbit about the
L1 position.

---

The L1 space station also serves as a communications relay for all near-side lunar radio and television messages. There is no L2 station, because its transmissions would interfere with the extremely sensitive radio telescope search for extraterrestrial intelligence underway at the far-side Star City observatory. All communications with far-side bases are carried by fiber-optic cables along the ground.

It is interesting to note that the Moon cannot have communications satellites in synchronous orbit, as the Earth does, because the synchronous orbit for the Moon is at the distance of the Earth! The orbits of lunar-synchronous commsats would be so perturbed by Earth's gravity that they would inevitably crash into the Earth.

**Site Selection**

After nearly ten years of exploring the Moon, both the United States and the Soviet Union finally decided to establish permanent lunar bases.

Several factors came into play in selecting a site for lunar surface operations. Among the most important was the amount of rocket energy necessary to reach the site. It is easiest, and therefore least expensive in terms of rocket propellant and money, to land close to the lunar equator. Even with a "first generation" lunar oxygen plant supplying 150 metric tons of oxygen for rocket propulsion per month from the American base at Alphonsus, propellant costs remained an important consideration in selecting sites for permanent bases.

The Russians, who had concentrated their explorations in the Mare Imbrium–Oceanus Procellarum area, selected the crater Aristarchus as the site of their permanent base, which they named Lunagrad. While Aristarchus is far to the northwest on the Moon's near side (24°N, 48°W), and therefore not as easily reached as a more equatorial location, it offered several offsetting advantages.

Prime among Aristarchus's attractions was the fact that the crater is the site of lunar outgassing. That is, from time to time, gases from the interior of the Moon seep through cracks in the crater's floor and escape into space. The gases are very diffuse; they would be regarded as a good vacuum on Earth. But they are evidence that volatiles* such as carbon and nitrogen exist beneath Aristarchus's floor, in the form of methane and ammonia. Deep-drilling efforts are seeking water, either in the form of ice or as hydrated compounds.

Thus Aristarchus represented, to the Soviets, a logical site for finding lunar resources that are important for human life support. In addition, their extensive explorations of the Mare Imbrium region showed that other important natural resources exist there in abundance, including metals such as titanium, aluminum, magnesium, and iron, which are valuable construction materials.

---

*Volatile, as the word is used at Moonbase, means any substance that would easily boil away during daylight on the lunar surface. Since carbon does not exist in solid form in the Moon's rocks and is found only as a constituent of methane gas ($CH_4$), it is considered to be a volatile.

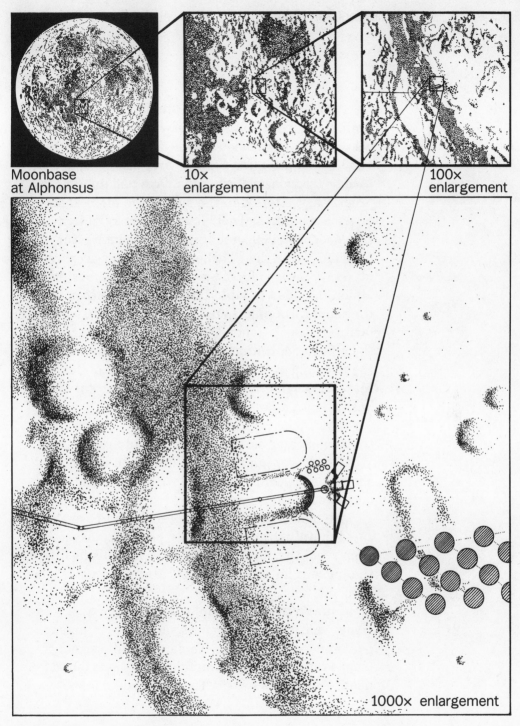

Moonbase
at Alphonsus

10× enlargement

100× enlargement

1000× enlargement

MOONBASE LOCATION AT ALPHONSUS

Moreover, Aristarchus's proximity to the lunar limb (the edge of the Moon, as viewed from Earth) was seen by the Soviets as another advantage. Since 1959, when the Luna 3 probe first photographed the Moon's far side, the Russians have had an almost proprietary interest in the side of the Moon that never faces Earth. Their first circumnavigation of the Moon, in 2009, reconfirmed their interest in the far side. While their earliest temporary bases were all on the near side, it was clear that the Soviet Union intended to build far-side bases as soon as they could. Having their major center at Aristarchus facilitated such a move, and within three years of the official dedication of Lunagrad at Aristarchus, the Russians established Zvezdagrad (Star City) at Mare Moscoviense. As its name implies, Star City is basically an astronomical center.

The Americans chose the crater Alphonsus as the site of their permanent base, and invited the Western European nations, China, and Japan to share the base (and its costs) with them. Thus was born Moonbase.

Alphonsus already had a temporary base, dedicated mainly to the facility for producing oxygen from regolith soil. The decision to use this facility as the nucleus for the permanent Moonbase made sound economic sense.

Like Aristarchus, Alphonsus is the site of occasional venting of noble gases such as neon and argon, and other volatiles. To date, small pockets of trapped methane and ammonia have been found beneath Alphonsus's floor. These provide minor amounts of needed volatiles such as hydrogen, carbon, and nitrogen.

Alphonsus's location at 13°S, 3°W makes it an economical location as far as transportation from Earth is concerned. The crater floor is traced by rilles, sinuous cracks and chains of craterlets that are associated with subsurface formations of volatiles. Although on the "shore" of Mare Nubium, Al phonsus is also close to the highland area that dominates the landscape between Nubium and the Mare Nectaris region to the east. Thus Alphonsus is close to both of the two types of ores found on the Moon: the basalts of a major mare and the anorthosites of the highlands.

**The "Bootstrap" Years**

The American decision to establish a permanent base on the Moon was made for a variety of scientific, economic, and political reasons. Although the bitter years of the Cold War were far behind both East and West, the fact that the Soviet Union was on its way to establishing Lunagrad no doubt prodded American leaders in both government and private industry. The main justification for a permanent Moonbase was economic: further exploration of the Moon and development of lunar resources could be supported much more inexpensively if lunar resources themselves could be used for life support, fuel, and structural material. The cost of creating a permanent base on the Moon was seen as less than the costs of continuing to supply all the needs of lunar exploration teams by transporting their supplies and equipment from Earth.

Moreover, lunar resources were also becoming critically important to space operations closer to Earth.

The earlier explorations of the lunar surface were facilitated in no small degree by the first-generation oxygen production plant that provided lunar oxygen for spacecraft propulsion. Lunar oxygen was also vitally important to the manufacturing operations going on in LEO, where zero-gravity processing of pharmaceuticals, crystals, and electronics components were creating a new industrial capability.

Earth-orbiting factories, however, had reached a bottleneck. The costs of lifting raw materials from the Earth to the orbital facilities imposed a high price on the products they manufactured. Even with lunar oxygen lowering the costs of transportation and life support in orbit, the LEO factories were strictly limited in their capabilities as long as they had to bring their raw materials up from Earth's surface. If raw materials could be supplied from the Moon, their price would drop by a factor of twenty—after amortizing the cost of setting up the lunar mining and launch facilities.

But while the driving motivation behind establishing Moonbase was the economic rationale of supplying raw materials to Earth-orbiting factories, the first half-decade of Moonbase's existence was spent almost entirely in building Moonbase itself. Except for oxygen exported to LEO, virtually every ounce of material and hour of manpower went into creating the base.

These were the bootstrap years, when construction engineers and swarms of teleoperated machines

dug into the floor of Alphonsus and built the structures that now dot its surface. Transfer rockets
landed virtually every day, disgorging equipment,
supplies, and personnel. The lunar oxygen facility
was doubled in size, then doubled again. A second
oxygen facility was built, in conjunction with a met-
als-processing plant on the outer rim of Alphonsus.
The electrically powered mass driver, a 4-kilometer-
long (approximately 2.5 miles-long) catapult, was
built on the plain of Mare Nubium. It launches payloads of ore toward Earth orbit at a price of a mere
few pennies of electricity per pound.

Moonbase's major structure, the Main Plaza, is
an elongated arched construct built entirely of lunar
concrete and reinforcing steel (except for the win
dows) and covered over with rubble from the regolith.
Built along the western inner face of Alphonsus's
ringwall mountains, the Main Plaza vault is 600
meters long (nearly 2,000 feet) and 75 meters high
(about 250 feet). Within the Main Plaza are the 15-
story Moonbase headquarters building, the shopping
arcade, the theater, and a variety of recreational
centers.

Corridors were driven through the subsurface
rock beneath the Main Plaza to a depth of 35 meters
(nearly 115 feet). Living quarters and working areas
are located along these corridors. Subsurface corridors also connect the Main Plaza to the spaceport, so
that passengers can go to and from the rocket vehicles without the need to walk on the surface in space
suits.

Originally it was suggested that small nuclear

# MAIN PLAZA CONSTRUCTION SEQUENCE

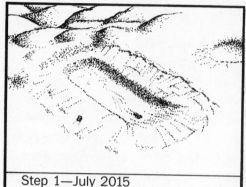

Step 1—July 2015
Clear and excavate site.

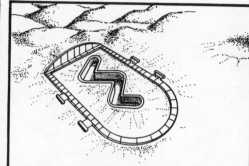

Step 2—December 2015
Emplace foundation and retaining walls.

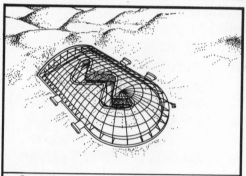

Step 3—December 2016
Erect metal structural truss.

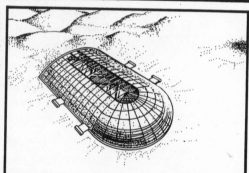

Step 4—April 2018
Install precast lunar concrete sections.

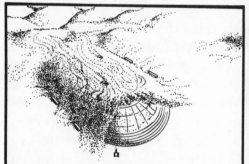

Step 5—October 2018
Cover with 6 meters of lunar regolith.

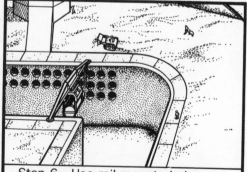

Step 6—Use rail-mounted plasma torch (mounted on crane) to cut habitation areas in "canyon" walls.

devices could be used to blast out the necessary habitation space beneath the surface. This was rejected on several grounds. First, nuclear explosives are prohibited on the Moon. Second, even if the necessary legal waivers could have been obtained, a nuclear explosive would have contaminated the proposed habitation space with significant amounts of radioactivity. Finally, seismologists pointed out that explosions in the kiloton range might have deleterious effects on the subsurface formations of gas pockets that honeycomb the interior of Alphonsus.

Instead of explosives, therefore, Moonbase's subsurface habitation areas were carved out with microwave beams and plasma torches that crumbled and even dissolved the rock. The underground spaces were made airtight by lining the rock with plastic sheets, heat-sealed to one another, before construction began. The entire working area was kept airtight even as mining teams extended the habitation space. While the digging was still going on, construction crews were building the living and working quarters in the areas already cleared.

Among the most massive and expensive pieces of equipment delivered from Earth to Moonbase were the base's original nuclear power generators. These were thermoelectric reactors capable of delivering 10,000 kilowatts each. Nuclear generators were chosen because they offered the highest output of power per weight, less than ten pounds per kilowatt, including the nuclear reactor, its shielding, and the radiators necessary to get rid of the excess heat it generated. The nuclear reactors were buried in the far side of the crater's ringwall and still provide electricity for Moonbase during the 350-hour-long lunar night.

It was during these bootstrap years that Moonbase initiated a major effort to use solar energy to produce electricity. Large tracts of Mare Nubium and the floor of Alphonsus were designated to be solar energy farms. Automated solar-cell factories were developed and mounted on crawlers. They plodded across the regolith, scooping up loose topsoil and processing its silicon into solarvoltaic cells that convert sunlight directly into electricity. The cells were then deposited on the ground.

Today these automated factories are still at work, far beyond the horizon as seen from the highest crest of Alphonsus's ringwall. They make Alphonsus's floor glitter in the sunlight. The solar energy farms produce all of Moonbase's electricity during the lunar day. Excess electrical power is now stored in large superconducting coils, for use during the night cycle or for emergencies. However, because of Moonbase's continuing expansion, the need for electrical power is constantly growing.

The solar energy farms are now tended by automated vehicles which sweep accumulated dust from the solar cells and repair the damage caused by occasional micrometeorite impacts.

While electrical power was a vital requirement for Moonbase, something even more basic was needed before the base could ever hope to be successful:

Food.

**Combined Aquaculture/ Agriculture**

The average human adult consumes roughly a kilogram (2.2 pounds) of food and water each day. To continually import this quantity of supplies from Earth would have meant that Moonbase would always be too small and too dependent to become a viable community on its own. The economic success of Moonbase depended on its being able to feed its population on homegrown foods.

During the bootstrap years, therefore, an intense effort was made to develop productive lunar farms. This required (among other things) a heavy importation of nitrogen from Earth, mainly in the form of ammonia, for use as fertilizer. Nitrogen is still a major import, although Moonbase's constant efforts to conserve water and volatiles, and locate alternate sources of these precious resources, have reduced the imports from Earth to a fraction of their earlier levels.

The farms were established underground, as was most of the rest of the base. At first the farms were lighted entirely by sunlight during daylight hours, and artificial lighting during the long lunar night. The sunlight was provided through filtered light shafts that reached from the surface to the caverns where the crops were being grown.

Five years of experimentation showed that artificial lighting provides more efficient crop productivity, because the wavelengths (color) of the lighting can be adjusted to suit the particular crops being grown. Long-term studies are still underway to determine the optimum trade-off between the use of filtered sunlight and the cost of the electricity to produce artificial lighting.

Most of the farming sections are maintained in an atmosphere that is high in carbon dioxide. Human attendants can work in these areas in their shirt-sleeves but require lightweight breathing masks. Experiments are underway to determine the optimum mix of air pressure and content for the various Moonbase crops.

Although it takes a considerable expenditure of time, manpower, and energy to carve out the large areas necessary for expanding the farms, all of Moonbase's agriculture is located underground, with the exception of a few small experimental plots in domes on the surface. In addition to being safer for the human workers tending the crops, keeping the farms underground protects the crops from radiation that might cause deleterious mutations. The rate of radiation-induced mutation is closely monitored in the surface experimental stations.

Regolith soil, however, is used for the underground farms. "Moondust" makes excellent farming soil; it is rich in trace elements that are often lacking in terrestrial farmlands, particularly those that have been under intense cultivation for centuries. Earthworms and other organisms that help to turn barren soil into productive farmland have been imported from Earth, and are now specially nurtured and bred in Moonbase's agricultural laboratories.

The earliest Moonbase "crop" was yeast, which is an extremely efficient source of protein. The protein was processed into various forms, known popularly by Moonbasers as "Moonburgers," "Lunasteak," and "Vic's Veggies" (after the nutritionist, Alfred Victor, who ran the yeast production facility at the time). Later, soybeans became a staple crop; not only did they provide a wider variety of processed proteins, but they also renitrogenated the soil in which they were grown.

## LUNAR LEGENDS: MOONDUST MAKES PLANTS GROW

According to a legend that harks back to the original Apollo program of the 1970 era, "Moondust"—the fine powder of the lunar regolith—has an almost magical effect on plant growth.

The legend has it that a technician at NASA's Johnson Space Center, outside Houston, surreptitiously sprinkled a bit of "Moondust" from the samples returned by the Apollo astronauts onto some plants he kept on the windowsill of his laboratory. The plants sprouted almost miraculously.

It is well-known that lunar soil contains many metallic and mineral trace elements that are nutrients for plant growth. In many terrestrial farmlands, especially those that have been used for centuries, these nutrients have been depleted and must be replaced by artificial fertilizers. Lunar soil is inherently fertile, although it must be enriched with water and microecological organisms such as earthworms before it becomes truly suitable for farming.

While water was a scarce and vitally important resource at Moonbase, experiments conducted on Earth proved that aquaculture—intensive production of protein-rich fish, shrimp, and algae—could improve the yield of lunar agriculture if developed together with the farms. Fed by human waste products (including carbon dioxide), the aquaculture systems yield oxygen, protein, vegetable matter, and irrigation water rich in nutrients. The combined aquaculture/agriculture systems now yield more than 200 tons of foodstuffs per acre per year.

Today, in addition to basic grains, legumes, and leafy vegetables, Moonbase's farms also produce meat products such as rabbit, pork, goat, and chicken. Seafood includes the trout, catfish, and shrimp of the original aquaculture stations, plus a growing amount of luxury items such as lobsters and shellfish.

Genetic engineers have developed special breeds of several crops that grow faster and produce more usable foodstuffs for the amount of light energy and fertilizers applied to them. They are now studying the possibilities of adapting Moonbase's animal stock to yield more meat per input of food.

The farms feed not only Moonbase's human population; lunar agricultural wastes feed Moonbase's growing plastics industry, as well. (See the "Moonrocks and Diamonds" chapter, p. 132 for details).

**Dedication of Moonbase**

Although the construction of Lunagrad actually began before the American decision to build a permanent lunar base, once the Moonbase program began and the Western allies agreed to join the effort, progress on Moonbase far outpaced the Russian effort on Lunagrad.

Officially, Moonbase was declared operational on 20 July 2020, eleven months before Lunagrad was officially opened.

Orlando Chavez became the first American President to visit Moonbase during his or her term of office. President Chavez officially dedicated Moonbase, in his words, "on behalf of the United States, our great friends in Western Europe, Japan, and China, and all the people of the Earth and the Moon."

# Moonbase Today

Moonbase is more than a growing community on the Moon. It is an example of a new experiment in government. Men and women from dozens of different nations live and work together at Moonbase, under laws that they themselves enact and administer.

The overriding goal of Moonbase is self sufficiency. Not merely in the physical sense of being independent of Earth for supplies and equipment, but in the political sense of having our people govern themselves.

**Moonbase Inc.**

Because Moonbase was created by an alliance of fifteen national governments, it became clear even before the first construction crew started work on the base that no single nation could claim control or sovereignty over it. Therefore, a private corporation was created—Moonbase Inc.—in which the major stock owners are the governments of the fifteen nations that originally financed construction of Moonbase: Australia, Belgium, Canada, China, Denmark, France, Germany, Great Britain, Ireland, Italy, Japan, the Netherlands, Spain, Sweden, and the United States.

Other significant stockholders in Moonbase Inc. include many of the larger multinational corporations, many of which have participated in the construction of Moonbase itself and in its operations.

Each employee of Moonbase is entitled to shares of the corporation stock, based on salary level and bonuses earned.

**The Governing Council**

While the corporate management has responsibility for all Moonbase operations, the men and women actually living at the base have the right to enact rules and regulations governing all phases of community activities. Any employee can be elected to the Moonbase Governing Council; the term of office is six months. This is strictly a voluntary position, with no financial remuneration. However, a Council member may be allowed time off from his or her job to conduct Council affairs without loss of pay.

The Council elects its own officers, and is responsible only to the voters of Moonbase. The Council can also negotiate with the management of Moonbase Inc. concerning matters of the workplace, such as safety, job performance criteria, and salary levels. In almost every respect, the Council is the government of Moonbase.

As a Moonbase employee, you are expected to vote in the Council elections. You should be prepared to participate in the governing of Moonbase and may want to run for the Council yourself. For more information, contact your local Council representative or check the seminars on citizenship and politics offered regularly by the Education Division.

**Moonbase Organization**

Moonbase Inc. is a not-for-profit corporation. At the end of each fiscal year, any accumulated surplus is reinvested in the research and exploration budget.

Moonbase's administration is composed of several major departments, each of which are in turn composed of divisions.

The *Department of Management* is responsible

for the overall operation of Moonbase. Within this department are the Administration, Human Resources, Contracts, Education, Finance, Materiél, Security, and Public Relations Divisions. The Governing Council advises the Department of Management and frequently negotiates with its divisions.

The *Department of Health and Safety* includes the Environmental Control Division, Life Support Division, Safety Division, and Water Allotment Board. This department also operates and manages Moonbase Hospital. In conjunction with medical researchers from the Research Program Office (see below), Moonbase Hospital is a vital center for long-term studies of the physical and psychological effects of living in a low-gravity, manmade environment.

The Life Support Division manages and administers Moonbase's agricultural programs.

The *Department of Technical Services* supports the operations of the major industrial and research facilities of Moonbase. Its divisions include Engineering Support, Technical Information, Transportation, Construction, Exploration, and Program Management.

There are four major industrial and research Program Offices currently in operation at Moonbase:

Mining and Manufacturing, which includes processing raw materials such as oxygen, silicon, and metals, as well as manufacturing finished products such as metal alloys, electronics components and systems, spacecraft assemblies, etc. Approximately seventy percent of such materials and products are exported to the Earth or to stations in Earth orbit. The remainder are used by Moonbase.

Space Transportation. Moonbase and the L1

space station service more than 65 percent of the manned and unmanned missions to deep space. Since 2017, all manned planetary missions have been supplied with lunar oxygen, either from Moonbase or Lunagrad.

Tourism. Last year nearly three thousand tourists visited Moonbase, bringing in a total of almost US $50 million. Typically, tourists are either honeymooners, small families with children aged 10 to 20, or retired couples. Tourist stays average two weeks.

Exploration and Research are major efforts at Moonbase. Physical, social, and medical scientists from every major university on Earth have come to the Moon to undertake studies that range from astronomy to psychology, from seismology to osteopathy. Moonbase University, staffed by permanent lunar residents, offers teaching positions to visiting scientists and scholars.

**Base Layout**

Moonbase consists of the main habitation and administrative center at Alphonsus, research facilities at various locations, and several outlying mining and industrial operations, mainly grouped near Alphonsus. The main landing and launch center for transportation to and from the L1 space station and/or Earth vicinity, popularly called the spaceport, is on the floor of Alphonsus just outside the Main Plaza. The electrical mass-driver facility for launching cargo payloads—mainly ores—is situated at the prime mining center on the eastern shore of Mare Nubium. A cable car system connects the Main Plaza and the spaceport with the operations on Mare Nubium, across Alphonsus's ringwall.

The Main Plaza is Moonbase's shopping and entertainment center. Numerous private shops offer a variety of luxury goods imported from Earth, together with items ranging from furniture to jewelry crafted by Moonbase inhabitants. The Moonbase Theater presents drama, dance, and musical offerings regularly. Performances by Moonbase personnel are usually either free or bear only a nominal charge to defray the actual costs. Ticket prices for performances by artists from Earth, however, can be very expensive despite the subsidies paid by Moonbase Inc. for "imported talent."

MOONBASE AREA PLAN

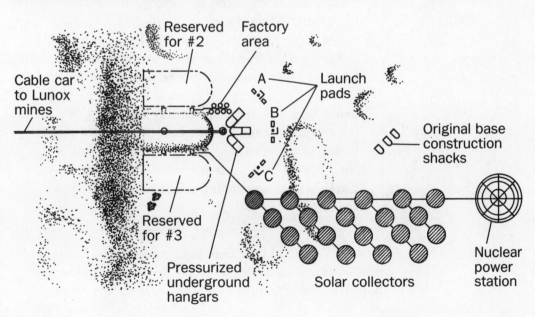

LUNAR LEGENDS:
THE UNDERGROUND ECONOMY

Moonbase Inc. maintains fully stocked stores that carry a wide range of consumer products, and private entrepreneurs have opened more than a dozen shops and two restaurants at Moonbase. Still, the permanent and visiting residents engage in a considerable amount of bartering and trade among themselves. This is often called "the underground economy," partly as a pun on the fact that Moonbase is an underground community.

Moonbase residents are entitled to bring a certain amount of personal goods from Earth, and often some of these goods are deliberately chosen for their value in trade. One woman, for example, carried 10 kilograms (22 pounds) of Venetian glass beads with her. Once at Moonbase she started a brisk trade in this kind of jewelry, so brisk that other residents began fashioning similar beads out of lunar glass. Management had to step in when it was discovered that a significant amount of the high-quality glass intended for export to Earth was disappearing into the underground economy.

Below the Main Plaza are five levels of living and working quarters. Vertical access is provided by power ladders, freight elevators, and ramps. (Stairs have been found to be hazardous to newcomers who are not acclimatized to one-sixth $g$; therefore, no stairs are allowed in Moonbase.)

Living quarters are on Levels 3 and 4. Level 1 is for life support machinery and warehousing. Levels 2 and 5 are offices and laboratories.

All sections of Moonbase are color-coded, and wall maps are provided in each corridor section. In addition, electronic directional markers are being installed in corridor floors. These can be accessed either by the wall telephone terminals or by pocket communicators.

Wherever feasible, greenstrips of living grass and shrubbery have been installed in the corridors. Each corridor also has a clearly marked lane for vehicular traffic—roller skates and skateboards can be used only in the marked lanes.

**Crawlers, Hoppers, Lobbers, and Trolleys**

Travel from the main habitation area to outlying facilities or other bases can be carried out in four ways.

*Crawlers* are wheeled, tracked, or multi-legged vehicles used for transport on the lunar surface. They can be adapted to a wide variety of purposes: bulldozers, back hoes, cargo haulers, personnel and/ or equipment carriers—even racing vehicles! Each year between Christmas and New Year's Day, Moonbase's personnel sponsor a cross-country race, usually across Mare Nubium to the Fra Mauro region, the crater Opelt, or similar destinations.

Crawlers can be operated in shirtsleeves. Their life support systems can go without replenishment for twenty-four hours or more. (During the annual cross-country race, these systems are augmented to serve for longer durations.) Crawler cabins are shielded against normal cosmic and solar wind radiation, but are not capable of withstanding the radiation from a major solar flare. Therefore crawlers are not allowed to be operated farther than a two-hour radius from an underground shelter.

*Hoppers* are small rocket-powered platforms capable of transporting up to three persons for distances of up to 50 kilometers (approximately 30 miles).

The rocket motors employ powdered lunar aluminum as their fuel and lunar oxygen as oxidizer. Hoppers are used mainly for high-speed transport of personnel or key equipment to various facilities.

Hoppers are not recommended for use in craters smaller than one kilometer in diameter, or in mountainous areas where suitable landing sites may not be found. Even in one-sixth gravity, a crash may result in serious injuries or fatality.

*Lobbers.* To facilitate longer-distance travel, ballistic rockets have been developed from the basic OTV configuration. Somewhat like a scaled-up hopper, these lobbers (the term comes from the game of tennis) can carry heavy payloads on a ballistic trajectory across distances of thousands of kilometers.

Like the hoppers, lobbers take off vertically. Because there is no air on the Moon, and therefore no aerodynamic forces on a flying vehicle, hoppers and lobbers alike stay in the same orientation as they fly along their ballistic trajectories. They land the same

*Short-range surface vehicles (0–50 Km range)*

MOONBASE AT ALPHONSUS

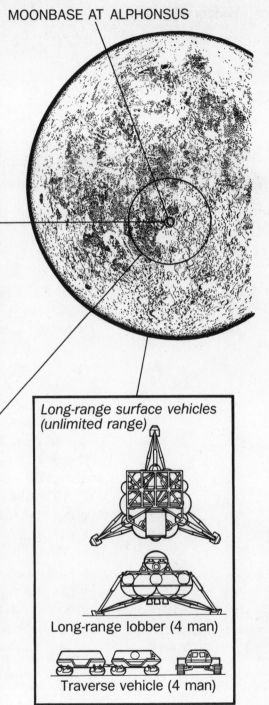

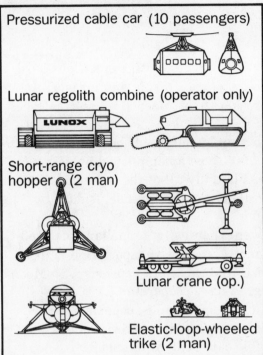

Pressurized cable car (10 passengers)

Lunar regolith combine (operator only)

Short-range cryo hopper (2 man)

Lunar crane (op.)

Elastic-loop-wheeled trike (2 man)

*Medium-range surface vehicles (0–500 Km range)*

Robot surface explorer

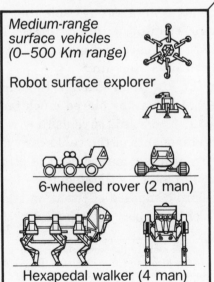

6-wheeled rover (2 man)

Hexapedal walker (4 man)

*Long-range surface vehicles (unlimited range)*

Long-range lobber (4 man)

Traverse vehicle (4 man)

**53**

way they took off, vertically, with a small on-board computer keeping the craft stable and measuring the amount of rocket thrust needed to land softly on the ground.

The first circumnavigation of the Moon, by the Soviet team in 2005, was accomplished by using a lobbing vehicle. Virtually all of the transportation to and from Star City, on the far side, is done by lobbers.

*Trolleys.* Even when using propellants derived from lunar resources, rocket transportation is inefficient energy-wise, and therefore expensive. So Moonbase and Lunagrad have cooperated for the past eight years on a system of cable-suspended electrically driven vehicles, popularly called trolleys.

Like the cable cars that go up mountains or across chasms and rivers on Earth, the lunar trolleys are suspended from a strong cable that is supported by pillars set into the lunar surface. Thus there is no need to prepare and maintain a roadway across the rugged lunar terrain.*

Thanks to the low lunar gravity, the supporting pillars for the system can be placed much farther apart, and need not be as massive as they would be on Earth. All components of the cable car system are manufactured from lunar materials. The pillars are lunar concrete, reinforced with steel from lunar iron ore. The cables are composed of titanium and aluminum. They not only support the traveling "trolleys,"

---

*Terrain* obviously has its roots in the word *terra*, meaning Earth. Since our expansion to the Moon and Mars, however, the word has come to mean the surface of whichever planetary body is under discussion.

but also carry fiber-optic communications cables.

Each trolley car is a self-contained life support module, capable of withstanding a crash onto the lunar surface and supporting up to twenty people for several days. Each car is also equipped with four emergency hard suits, radio and laser communications systems, and automatic beacons to signal rescuers.

To date, no trolley has suffered any accident involving more than a minor delay.

Cable car lines have been completed between Moonbase and Lunagrad, and between these major centers and more than thirty percent of their respective outlying facilities. Moonbase Inc. has been contracted by the Soviet government to erect a cable system that will link Lunagrad with Star City, in the Mare Moscoviense, on the far side.

**Navigating on the Moon**

Navigation on the Moon depends on radio beacons. Antennas atop the Alphonsus ringwall crest transmit location "fixes" for persons on the crater floor or outside on the Mare Nubium. The space station at L1 also beams navigation signals that can be picked up by the radios in hard suits anywhere on the Moon's near side.

Earth-style navigation is impossible on the Moon. Magnetic compasses do not point north. They point, instead, to the nearest large mare—which are underlain by mascons (mass concentrations) of dense rock. The mascons' intrinsic magnetic fields are strong enough to mask the extremely weak overall magnetic field of the Moon.

Nor can you navigate by the stars, unless you know that the lunar north pole does not point to Polaris, the pole star of Earth. Instead, it points in the direction of Draco, a comparatively dim constellation of stars that sprawls between the Big and Little Dippers (Ursa Major and Minor). Because the Moon wobbles on its axis much more than the Earth does, its north pole wavers considerably and does not point toward a specific star for more than a dozen years or so at a time.

## Transportation to/from Earth

Earthbound flights leave Moonbase from the main spaceport in Alphonsus every week, on a regular schedule that is easily available at any computer terminal.

Normally, flights Earthward entail two transfers: one at the L1 space station in lunar orbit and the second at an Earth-orbiting station. Direct flights—that is, flights to a space station in LEO—are conducted only for emergency reasons.

All flights from Earth also normally transfer at LEO and L1. Direct flights from LEO to Moonbase are made only for emergencies.

Your flight to Moonbase is, of course, prepaid by Moonbase Inc. Your return flight Earthward, when your contracted work period is finished, will also be furnished free of charge by the corporation. All transportation undertaken for approved job-related reasons is free. Recreational transportation on the Moon can be obtained either at a discount or free, depending on specific circumstances. The Transportation Division regularly publishes schedules and fares on the Moonbase electronic bulletin board. Transportation to Earth, for reasons other than medical or personal emergency, must be paid for by the employee.

# Job Guidelines

Your work at Moonbase will be challenging and demanding, but well within your capabilities. You have already passed some of the most rigorous screening tests on Earth and have amply demonstrated your job skills and motivation. Now you are ready to work on the Moon.

Moonbase has a high reputation for excellence in everything we do—excellence that is created by our people. Outstanding people. People like you.

*Note*: In all discussions in this section of the Manual, when we speak of Moonbase we include the L1 space station, which, although not Moonbase property, is administered by Moonbase Inc. All employee benefits, responsibilities, and regulations that apply to Moonbase itself apply equally to the L1 space station.

**Job Opportunities**
You already have a specific position waiting for you at Moonbase. The following list shows our major job categories, so that you can familiarize yourself with the jobs that your coworkers and neighbors will hold. Eventually, you may want to transfer to another position, or upgrade your education and/or skill level to attain a better position.

Job categories include:

<u>Department of Management</u>. Administrators, administrative assistants, secretaries, data manage ment specialists, attorneys specializing in contracts, patents, international law, and international commerce, accountants, financial planners, insurance specialists, personnel specialists, psychologists, teachers, educational administrators, interactive TV

producers, interactive TV technicians, purchasing agents, marketing and sales specialists, inventory managers, security specialists, public relations specialists, writers/editors (for print, radio, and TV), photographers, art directors, TV cameramen, and communications engineers.

<u>Department of Health and Safety</u>. Environmental scientists, engineers, and technicians; medical doctors, nurses, and hospital technicians; dental doctors, nurses, and hygienists, physical therapists, sports therapists, nutritionists, agricultural engineers and farm workers; biologists (macro and molecular); genetic engineers and technicians; life support engineers and technicians; electrical engineers (power); hydraulic specialists (i.e., plumbers); environmental control engineers and technicians; radiation scientists and engineers; common law adjudicators; ombudsmen.

<u>Department of Technical Services</u>. Engineer categories include structural, civil, aerodynamic, electronic, electrical, electrical (power), mining, rocket propulsion, design, and test. Other categories include data management, information services, teleoperator design and control, computer analysis, Artificial Intelligence design and programming, mapping, geology, transportation management, factory design and layout, and program administration.

<u>Mining and Manufacturing Program Office</u>. Geologists, geochemists, mining engineers, factory managers, machinists, teleoperators, computer analysts, metallurgists, plastics chemists, chemical engineers, cryogenics engineers and technicians, crystallographers, electronics engineers and technicians, produc-

tion engineers and technicians, optics engineers and technicians.

Space Transportation Program Office. Engineer and technician categories include astronautics, spacecraft design, rocket propulsion, electronics, life support, logistics, teleoperation, and computers (with special requirements for Artificial Intelligence programming, control, and analysis).

Tourism Program Office. Hotel management, recreational services, food and beverage services, tour guides, paramedical specialist, paralegal specialists, and psychologists.

Exploration and Research Program Office. Scientists, engineers, and technicians in the fields of astronomy, astrophysics, geophysics, plasma physics, selenology, seismology, particle physics, theoretical physics, astrochemistry, radio astronomy, the search for extraterrestrial intelligence (SETI), planetary astronomy, chemistry (with emphasis on vacuum chemistry), low-gravity physiology, osteopathy, geriatrics, cardiovascular research, biology, plant and livestock genetics, and ecology.

Unskilled labor is done almost entirely by robots or computer-directed automated machinery, except where human personality is considered an important asset—as in several service categories in the Tourism Program Office.

Computer programming is done exclusively by Moonbase's AI systems; there is no job category for computer programmers, although many Moonbasers occasionally program computers themselves.

You have been assigned to a job that fits your skills, your education and—most important—your

own desires for challenge, opportunity, and fulfill-
ment. The results of the rigorous aptitude, physical,
and psychological screening tests you have already
passed show that you are the kind of person who is
seeking career advancement.

Moonbase wants and needs forward-looking people like you. Opportunities for furthering your education and upgrading your skill level are available to
every Moonbase employee. Your supervisor will be
glad to help you "move up the ladder." For the educational opportunities at Moonbase, see the "Education" section in this chapter.

**Pay and Benefits**

Outstanding people deserve outstanding rewards for
the work they do. Moonbase offers the best pay and
benefit programs anywhere in the solar system.

Your salary is the most direct reward you get
from your work. It is the key to your financial security and your standard of living. So we make certain
that you and all other Moonbase employees have the
finest salary opportunities available.

To accomplish this we have established salary
levels that are better than the salaries offered for
comparable jobs on Earth or aboard the space stations in LEO. And we add an automatic 25 percent
*lunar bonus* to each Moonbase employee's salary.
Your work at Moonbase will earn you more than
similar work elsewhere.

We continuously check to make certain that
each person's salary is fair in relation to everyone
else's, and continues to be fair in relation to that
person's individual job performance.

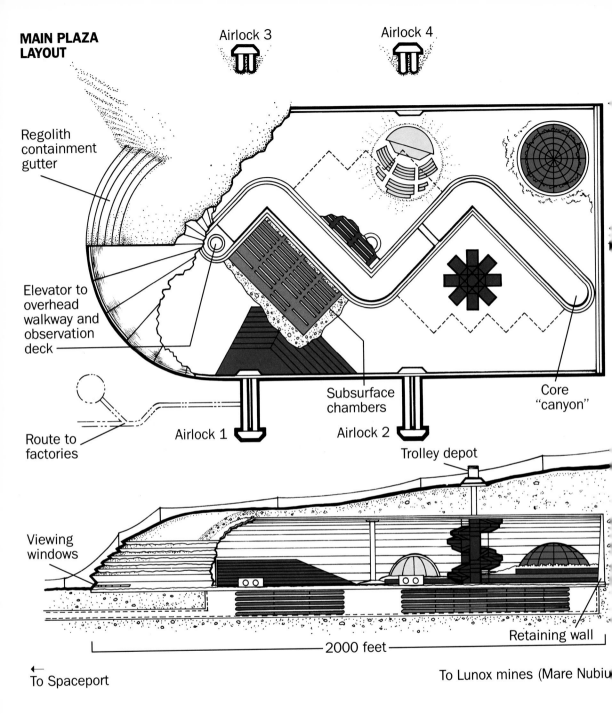

# MAIN PLAZA LAYOUT

Airlock 3

Airlock 4

Regolith containment gutter

Elevator to overhead walkway and observation deck

Route to factories

Airlock 1

Subsurface chambers

Airlock 2

Core "canyon"

Trolley depot

Viewing windows

2000 feet

Retaining wall

← To Spaceport

To Lunox mines (Mare Nubiu

## LEGEND

- ■ Residential
- ■ Research Laboratories
- ■ Life Support
- ☐ Entertainment
- ■ Moonbase Corporate Headquarters
- ■ Lunox Corporate Headquarters
- ■ Storage
- ■ General Office Retail Space
- ■ Reservoir

*Previous pages:*

1. Lift-off from Launch Pad #
2–3. Mountain-climbing on the Alphonsus Crater wall
4–5. Human-powered flight inside the Main Plaza
6–7. The Annual Cross-Count Crawler Race

All employees are paid once a month. You'll be paid on either the first, tenth, or twentieth of the month, depending on which date is closest to the day you actually began working at Moonbase. Salaries are deposited in your personal account even if that day falls on a weekend or holiday.

Since Moonbase is a virtually cashless community, your salary is deposited in your personal bank account. All purchases made at Moonbase are deducted from your account. You can transfer funds electronically to a bank on Earth or to the accounts of your family; all you need is a telephone and a voice-print identification to verify the transfer.

Taxes and Deductions. Moonbase's employees come from many different nations. While Moonbase exacts no taxes whatsoever on its employees, the governments of the nations that the employees come from *do* expect their citizens to pay taxes, even while working on the Moon. Therefore, each employee is taxed in accordance with the laws of his or her nation of citizenry. All deductions for taxes, personal medical insurance, retirement funds, etc, are itemized on each salary payment. Itemized statements are issued by computer and kept in the Human Resources Division's computer records. Hard copies can be made at any computer terminal equipped with a printer.

Special Bonuses. Since each Moonbase employee is salaried, there is no extra pay for overtime work. As a professional, you are expected to work on a goal-oriented rather than an hourly wage basis. Thus there is no overtime pay for working longer than a normal shift.

However, each supervisor is empowered to request special bonuses for special performance. Bonuses do not come automatically, but whenever a Moonbase employee "goes the extra mile" to get the job done, Moonbase recognizes such effort—and rewards it.

Employees who regularly work on the surface receive an additional bonus. Widely referred to in the base as "vacuum pay," such bonuses are recognition of the fact that working on the surface entails special risks and hazards.

Time Off with Pay. There are also many times of the year when you are away from work, to relax and have fun. Or to take care of special responsibilities. In most cases you will get full pay during such absences.

Under our vacation program, you are entitled to a full week's paid vacation after six months of working at Moonbase. While most employees choose to spend their vacation at Moonbase (there *is* a whole new world here to explore), others opt to return to Earth. This is permitted only if the employee and any persons travelling with him or her can pass the physical examination and be certified for Earth return.

If, after completing a year's employment, you renew your contract for another year, you will qualify for two week's vacation, which you can take at your discretion, with the approval of your supervisor. Employees who remain at Moonbase for longer periods get an additional week's vacation for each additional year of service, up to five years. Permanent lunar residents make special vacation arrangements with the Human Resources Division.

If a paid holiday falls within your vacation time, an extra paid day is added to your vacation.

Paid Holidays. Because Moonbase's people come from so many different nations and cultural heritages, we ask each new employee to select twelve holidays during the year and allow the employee those twelve days as paid holidays. The only restriction on this is that no holidays may run more than two consecutive calendar days.

If it is necessary for an employee to work during a day selected as a holiday, the employee will receive a holiday bonus equivalent to a full day's pay in addition to his or her regular pay for that day.

Pay for Other Absences. There is no sick leave at Moonbase. Your salary continues even if you are unable to work because of illness. However, if you are incapacitated for sixty consecutive days, Moonbase may terminate your employment contract and return you to your nation of origin on Earth.

If you need to take time off to fulfill personal obligations, Moonbase will continue to pay your salary in full, providing your supervisor approves your absence. Transportation costs to Earth and return may be paid in whole or in part by Moonbase, upon recommendation by your supervisor and review by the Human Resources Division.

**Benefit Program**    Moonbase provides the finest benefit program in the solar system. If you become ill, or are disabled temporarily or even permanently, Moonbase provides a wide range of financial protection for you and your family. These benefits cost you nothing, unless you wish to set aside a portion of your salary to increase the coverage of the medical, dental, retirement, and other programs that are automatically provided by Moonbase.

All medical costs associated with job-related illness or injury are paid by Moonbase. This includes the cost of transportation back to Earth, if necessary. Moonbase health insurance also protects your family: in most cases, the insurance covers the total cost of any illness or injury. You may add additional coverage for your dependents at a small cost, deducted automatically from your salary each month.

Coverage for you and your family begins the day you leave Earth for your job at Moonbase. It pays full costs of semiprivate hospital rooms for up to 365 days per admission, in most cases; all surgery fees and costs that are reasonable and customary; hospital costs and doctor's fees; up to six weeks of disability income benefits in maternity cases, as well as benefits for the newborn baby.

Coverage includes the cost of virtually every kind of medical care you and your family may need: medical X-rays, CAT scans and other tests, doctor's care, nursing care, outpatient care, emergency treatment, and many others.

Moonbase also provides a dental plan that offers the same kinds of coverage as the medical plan. Good dental care begins with prevention, and the dental plan pays for routine checkups. It also pays for fillings, inlays, crowns, extractions, oral surgery, gum treatment, and other types of dental care.

The dental plan does not cover elective orthodonture or other cosmetic dental procedures. However, you may elect to pay a small premium to add such coverage to your family dental plan.

**Insurance and Retirement**

Moonbase offers life and accident insurance as a basic part of your benefits. Life insurance benefits up to five times your annual salary are paid for by Moonbase; you can add to this coverage voluntarily through a small salary deduction. Accident insurance benefits are also paid totally by Moonbase.

Although most new Moonbase employees are far from retirement age, it is possible for any employee to begin a cooperative retirement plan, in which Moonbase matches any payments made by the employee.

**Education**

Moonbase encourages education in several ways.

Through our Educational Assistance Program, we pay for technical or managerial courses that will increase your skills and knowledge. Such courses may be given at Moonbase or attended by interactive video communication with schools on Earth. Moonbase repays up to 100 percent of your costs for approved courses, depending on the final grade you achieve.

The Scholarship Program pays up to 100 percent of the costs of tuition and lodging for the college education of any Moonbase employee, for each year the employee has actually worked at Moonbase.

Moonbase University is mainly a research center, rather than a teaching institution. Its permanent staff consists of permanent Moonbase residents, while the visiting faculty is made up of temporary employees and occasional guest lecturers specifically invited to Moonbase. Although no undergraduate instruction is offered at the University, graduate degrees can be obtained in fields such as low-gravity physiology, astronomy, selenography, and other areas associated with Moonbase's expertise. Moonbase University is accredited by more than fifty nations, including each of the fifteen major share holders in Moonbase Inc.

In addition, Moonbase provides a small but growing public educational system at the base. Starting with day care centers for preschool-age children, Moonbase's educational facilities include a complete grammar and high school (up to the age level of 17–18), and a range of adult education courses in subjects associated with Moonbase's business and industrial activities. Employees attend adult classes on their own time, unless specifically granted time off from their jobs by their supervisors.

Finally, there are many recreational adult classes given by Moonbase residents. These range from low-gravity dance to "first footprints" treks on the Moon's surface. Such recreational classes are entirely voluntary.

**Family Accommodations**

Moonbase does not encourage new employees to bring their families to the Moon. In fact, we actively discourage such a move.

Frankly, living on the Moon is such a unique experience that it takes the average newcomer weeks to adjust to the lunar environment and the conditions of his or her work. To ask an entire family to adjust to such conditions at the same time—especially a family that may include young children—is to invite extra problems.

In addition, living space at Moonbase is still at a premium, although we are expanding the living quarters under a vigorous program of growth.

Therefore, almost every new employee has agreed not to bring his or her immediate family to Moonbase.

However, employees who choose to extend their original one-year contracts, and persons who are allowed to live at Moonbase permanently, have every right to bring their immediate families to the Moon to live with them. Moonbase provides extra living quarters, schools, medical and dental care, and all other possible amenities for families.

Psychological Counseling. Because the Moon *is* a long way from Earth, and because the stresses of working in a new environment, often without family or friends nearby, can create difficulties, Moonbase provides free psychological counseling for all its employees. Such counseling is strictly confidential.

**Employment Contract**

As a condition of your employment at Moonbase, you will be required to sign an Employment Agreement, usually for a one-year term. A sample agreement is given in Appendix 2. *Read your agreement carefully.* Your Human Resources counselor will be happy to answer any questions you have about specific clauses or about your responsibilities under the agreement.

# Quality of Life

Living conditions at Moonbase are more conducive to good health than almost any place on Earth.

Although most of the base is underground, every effort has been made to make the living quarters, public areas, and work spaces as comfortable and Earthlike as possible.

**Shirtsleeve Environment**

Most of Moonbase is underground, so that it can be maintained in a shirtsleeve environment.

Temperatures on the surface of the Moon range from 134° C (273° F) at local noon to −153° C (−243° F) in the darkness of the two-week-long lunar night. By constructing Moonbase underground, these huge swings of temperatures can be avoided. Moonbase can be kept at a comfortable interior temperature with a minimum expenditure of energy.

There is no need for special protective clothing anywhere in the underground sections of the base.

The interior temperature is regulated to stay in the range between 20° C (68° F) and 24° C (75° F). The atmosphere is kept at an Earthlike pressure of 14.7 pounds per square inch throughout the base. It is composed of approximately 80 percent nitrogen and 20 percent oxygen, just as on Earth. However, because of the scarcity of water on the Moon, atmospheric humidity is kept quite low, well under 20 percent. Generally, the atmosphere inside Moonbase resembles that of the American southwest: imagine an area such as Phoenix, Tucson, or Albuquerque on a pleasant springtime day—without the air pollution!

Environmental control is quite rigorous. With more than two thousand people living in Moonbase, it is necessary to monitor the atmosphere constantly to guard against potential pollution. Environmental sensors have been placed in every room, corridor, and public area of Moonbase. They continuously record temperature, humidity, and contamination levels. These sensors are constantly monitored by specialists of the Environmental Control Division, who also dispatch humans and/or robots on random patrols of Moonbase's living and working areas to inspect the sensors and make on-the-scene evaluations of compliance with environmental regulations. The sensors also serve as smoke and fire detectors, and have helped save lives in emergencies.

Smoking is not prohibited at Moonbase, but it is strictly controlled. All public areas, including all corridors and work places, are strictly no-smoking areas. Smoking is permitted in one's private living quarters, and in special smoking lounges provided at certain locations adjacent to public areas and work places. Tobacco products can be brought to Moonbase only as part of an individual's personal cargo allowance. No sale of tobacco products is permitted anywhere in Moonbase.

Alcoholic beverages are sold at Moonbase shops and served in our restaurants. Narcotics and other stimulant/depressant drugs are strictly controlled. Alcohol or drug abuse can be grounds for dismissal. If in doubt concerning medicinal drugs, contact the Life Support Division's counselors.

**"Green" Policy**     Integrity of the atmosphere is ensured by the Life Support Division's multi-unit atmospheric regeneration systems. This equipment, which is triply redundant and designed to fail-safe, is installed in eight key locations in Moonbase, with back-up systems kept in reserve to meet any possible emergency contingency. The air regeneration systems consist of scrubbers and regenerators similar to those used aboard space stations and in spacecraft.

Because of Moonbase's large and growing size, however, and because we want our community to be as Earthlike as possible, Moonbase has embarked on a "Green" Policy. This means that green plants, ranging from ordinary grass to reasonably sized trees, are being planted wherever feasible.

Most of the public areas of Moonbase, such as the Main Plaza, have been planted with trees and shrubbery. Greenstrips of grass and flowering plants line many of the corridors and recreation areas.

Every member of Moonbase's growing population is encouraged to bring green plants to the base, and to send for more once here. This is an entirely voluntary decision, since it cuts into the limited mass allowance for personal items. However, to encourage the "Green" Policy, Moonbase offers a 50 percent mass allowance on all seeds and plants imported from Earth. Thus every kilogram of seeds or plants an employee brings to Moonbase is counted as only half a kilo in that individual's personal mass allowance.

The "Green" Policy requires a considerable allotment of precious water for the plants. However, this allotment was approved because: (1) Since "gray" (nonpotable) water can be used, there is no competition for drinking water; (2) the plants recycle the water provided them, so that it is not lost permanently; and (3) the advantages of the greenery outweigh the cost of the water provided.

In addition to making our underground community appear more Earthlike, the green plants help to recycle the atmosphere, converting carbon dioxide into breathable oxygen. As yet, however, there are not enough plants to take more than a minor fraction of the workload from the air regenerators.

*Note*: Persons who suffer severe allergies related to grasses and pollens are no longer considered qualified for employment at Moonbase unless their allergic symptoms can be controlled with antihistamines or other medication.

**Low-Gravity Living**

The Moon is one-quarter the size of the Earth, and lacks the heavy metals and massive inner core of our home world. Therefore, gravity at Moonbase is approximately one-sixth the surface gravity of Earth.

For the most part, this low gravity is a great benefit, and most Moonbase residents find it a pleasant experience.

Compared to most of the space stations, which are effectively at zero gravity, Moonbase's living conditions are much more Earthlike. No one has contracted the "space sickness" (Space Adaptation

Syndrome) that affects newcomers to a weightless environment. Living and working in one-sixth gravity is much easier than either Earth's full one $g$ or the zero-$g$ of the space stations.

Although everything weighs only one-sixth of its earthly equivalent on the Moon, there is still a definite up and down. The delicate balance mechanisms of the inner ear are not disturbed by the low gravity, as they are by the virtual absence of gravity aboard space stations. Eating, drinking, working, and all phases of living can be accomplished with only a minimum of orientation.

Walking in one-sixth $g$ does require some practice. Because our muscles are accustomed to working against the full gravity of Earth, newcomers to Moonbase tend to leap and bounce about until they become accustomed to their new environment. Generally this takes a day or so.

Once the newcomer adapts to the "lunar shuffle," as some have called the graceful, gliding walk that best suits one-sixth $g$, he or she finds that getting around Moonbase is not only easier than walking on Earth—it can be fun.

It takes a few more days to learn to coordinate other movements in one-sixth $g$. Pouring liquids can be especially interesting, and newcomers learn quickly that seemingly simple skills such as typing and athletic activities requiring hand–eye coordination will take some practice.

The low gravity has affected lunar architecture. There are no stairs at Moonbase, because of the difficulty in judging one's steps in one-sixth *g*: ramps, elevators, and power ladders are used instead. And virtually all Moonbase living quarters have ceilings of 5 meters (slightly more than 16 feet) height. Ceilings in public areas are a minimum of 8 meters (above 26 feet).

Roller skates and skateboards have become very popular in Moonbase, not merely for recreation but as an important means of transportation inside the base. We do not permit vehicular traffic inside the base, but individuals with skates can move through the corridors and public spaces with gratifying speed. This is becoming more important as Moonbase is enlarged, and distances from one section of the base to another continue to grow.

*Note:* Special skaters' lanes have been clearly labeled in all the major corridors and public areas. Whether on roller skates or skateboards, no one is allowed to skate anywhere except in the specially designated lanes. Collisions between skaters and pedestrians will be judged to be the fault of the skater unless it can be unequivocally established that the pedestrian was in the skating lane at the time of the accident.

**Exercise Policy**

While living in one-sixth gravity is generally beneficial, it can lead to some deterioration of the musculature unless corrective action is undertaken. Osteoporosis, which makes the bones brittle, can also result from a long-term low-gravity environment. For this reason, Moonbase has established a mandatory exercise policy for each resident of the base.

There are three medical/physical problems to be considered: cardiovascular deconditioning, general loss of muscle tone and strength, and osteoporosis. Although these problems are not as severe as those encountered in long-duration zero-gravity missions, they must be kept in mind by anyone who lives on the Moon for more than a few weeks and expects to return to Earth.

Therefore the Department of Health and Safety has established a policy of mandatory daily exercise. Each newcomer to Moonbase is provided with a personal exercise regime. Failure to comply with this regime can lead to dismissal and return either directly to Earth or to a space station for reconditioning.

Exercise periods are "shared time"; that is, half of each daily exercise period counts as paid employment time. The other half is part of the employee's personal time. All the exercise facilities and equipment are provided free of charge to all Moonbase residents. Recreational activities that have been approved by the Department of Health and Safety may be counted as exercise time, but not as paid employment time.

*Note:* Read carefully the terms of your group insurance agreement, so that you understand the conditions under which your employment contract may be penalized or terminated due to lack of compliance with the mandatory exercise policy.

**Radiation**      The most serious danger on the Moon is radiation,
most of which comes from the solar wind and cosmic
rays.

Earth's surface is protected from most forms of
damaging radiation by the geomagnetic field that di-
verts and traps charged-particle radiation, and by
the thick terrestrial atmosphere that absorbs much
of the remaining particles and rays. The Moon, however, has only a negligible atmosphere and magnetic
field. Therefore solar and cosmic radiation reach the
lunar surface unimpeded. This is another reason why
Moonbase is almost entirely underground, where the
lunar crust serves as an effective radiation shield.

Many Moonbase workers, however, perform their
jobs on the surface. They are provided radiation protection in the form of hardened space suits and
shielded surface vehicles and structures.

Not all radiation is dangerous. Light and heat
from the Sun, for example, are forms of radiation
that are not only beneficial but necessary for life to
exist. Even in Moonbase's underground sections,
great care is taken to bring in sunlight wherever
possible.

Damaging radiation consists mainly of energetic charged particles, such as electrons and protons,
and rays of pure energy, such as X-rays and gamma
rays. In general, the more energetic the particle or
ray, the more damage it can cause to body tissues.

A fairly steady *solar wind* of protons and electrons streams from the Sun at speeds of more than
320 kilometers (200 miles) per second. The protons in

the solar wind normally carry a kinetic energy of about 800 electron volts; the electrons, being almost 2,000 times lighter than the protons, carry far less energy.

But the Sun is not always placid. Every few days a solar disturbance will emit particles with energies of some five million electron volts, and at least once or twice a year a major solar flare will erupt and blast out particles of a billion electron volts or more. While most of these "storm clouds" of highly energetic particles do not reach the Earth–Moon area, those that do pose extreme hazards for human beings on the lunar surface. Fortunately, it is possible to detect such solar eruptions at least an hour before the bulk of the radiation cloud reaches the Moon.

*Warning:* When a radiation alert is sounded, all personnel on the surface *must* return below ground *immediately*. Failure to do so can result in fatal radiation dosages. Your employment contract and insurance policy specify that you will be held responsible for any resulting illness, injury, or death if you fail to respond to a properly issued radiation alert. This can result in loss of benefits for you and/or your survivors.

In addition to solar particulate radiation, there is a constant stream of energetic cosmic rays that originate in deep space, far beyond the solar system. Although they are called "rays" and "radiation," cosmic rays consist of subatomic particles, mostly protons plus a small percentage of bare nuclei of

heavier atoms. They have been accelerated to energies of more than 100 million electron volts by unknown processes deep in the interstellar vastness.
The most energetic cosmic "rays" are not stopped by
Earth's magnetic field or atmosphere; they penetrate
even into the deepest mines of Earth;. Naturally,
they also penetrate into the underground sections of
Moonbase. However, since the human race has been
exposed to this form of cosmic radiation for untold
eons, it is part of the natural background radiation
environment and is considered harmless.

Because the Moon lacks the heavier elements
that make up much of the Earth's bulk, the background level of radiation from rocks is lower on the
Moon than on Earth, and Moonbases's protective
shielding of lunar rock and soil actually keeps the
radiation level within the base slightly below the
natural background radiation levels on Earth.

**Living Quarters**  Arthur C. Clarke, the twentieth-century author and
futurist, was once asked, "How can you, living in the
tropical paradise of Sri Lanka, advocate living in the
totally artificial and enclosed environment of space
habitats?" Clarke replied, "That's a very good question. Perhaps you ought to ask it, though, of my good
friend Isaac Asimov. He lives in New York City!"

Many Earthbound people believe that living on
the Moon means living in a high-tech cave, always
enclosed underground in cramped, dreary, window-
less cells.

While all living quarters in Moonbase are indeed underground, they are far from cramped and dreary.

Living space is at a premium, however, although we are constantly expanding Moonbase in a vigorous but carefully planned program of growth.

Floorspace. Your initial living quarters will be a one-room apartment, slightly larger than the average studio apartment in major Earthside metropolitan centers such as Manhattan, Tokyo, or Moscow. While dimensions vary somewhat from one apartment to another, the average size is between 100 square feet (9.29 square meters) and 175 square feet (16.25 square meters). Married or cohabitating couples can make arrangements for two adjoining rooms with a connecting door.

Your furniture is provided by Moonbase. Basic furniture includes a sofabed, two endtables, a bookcase, a desk with chair, two occasional chairs, coffee table, and associated lamps. Each apartment is equipped with a functioning kitchen, which includes a foldout table and two chairs, and an ultrasonic dishwasher. Each apartment is also equipped with a bathroom, which includes toilet, shower stall, and sink.

Laundry facilities are provided in each section of Moonbase's living quarters. Ultrasonic clothes-washing machines are being installed in some apartments, but these luxury items will not be available in every apartment for some time to come.

Permanent Moonbase residents can expand their

living quarters into multi-room dwellings. The cost for drilling through the rock for such expansion is shared by Moonbase and the resident. Furniture for enlarged apartments is either purchased or made by the residents.

Personal Hygiene. Because water is precious on the Moon and electrical energy is abundant, Moonbase residents are encouraged to use the ultrasonic scrubbers provided in each apartment's bathroom in preference to showering. The scrubbers remove dirt and dead skin from the body's surface through ultrasonic vibrations.

Each Moonbase resident is granted a monthly water allowance, and may use that allotment of water in any way he or she chooses. Once the allotment is used the individual will receive no more water until the first of the next month. Appeals can be made to the Water Allotment Board, but only cases of extreme need or system failures attributable to Moonbase itself are grounds for a successful appeal.

Windows. Although all living quarters are underground, each apartment has a "window." Each apartment is furnished with a large wall-screen TV, capable of receiving all channels transmitted from the space station at L1—which includes practically every entertainment, information, and educational channel on Earth. The TV screen can also be used as a "window." Moonbase transmits live camera views of the lunar surface throughout the base, so that it is possible to see the surface from the comfort of your apartment.

Many residents also play videotapes of favorite Earthly scenes, providing their apartments with a "window" that looks out on a familiar terrestrial view.

Emergency Procedures. The doors to each apartment (and between adjoining apartments) are not airtight. However, in all corridors there are safety doors spaced approximately every 100 meters (roughly 300 feet). The safety doors are airtight and fireproof. They are closed automatically in case of fire, loss of air pressure, or other emergency.

If you are caught in your apartment or in a corridor when the safety doors are sealed shut, DO NOT PANIC. Emergency crews from the Department of Health and Safety are summoned automatically when the safety doors close. They can reach any part of Moonbase within three minutes. Telephones are available in every corridor section and in every apartment. Touch "1-1-1" for help.

In case of fire, remain in your apartment. Stay low to avoid smoke inhalation. Fire extinguishers are provided in each apartment, together with emergency breathing masks that contain a five-hour supply of oxygen, in case of air pressure loss. Automatic sensors will alert emergency rescue crews instantly, and help will reach you within a few minutes.

Emergency procedures are printed on the door of each apartment. Each workplace also has its emergency plan prominently displayed. Emergency drills are held monthly. Participation is mandatory.

**Recreation and
Entertainment**

Like any thriving community, Moonbase offers a wide spectrum of recreational and entertainment opportunities that are based mostly on the activities and interests of our residents, both temporary and permanent.

Music, Dance, Drama. Moonbase has its own Little Theater, Glee Club, Symphonic Ensemble, and Dance Troupe; all are composed entirely of local residents. While television provides access to every major entertainment channel on Earth (as well as news and educational channels), special direct links are frequently set up so that Moonbase's residents may view concerts, plays, dances, and other offerings from Earth.

In addition, performances by the best professional artists on Earth are regularly scheduled at Moonbase. The Philadelphia Orchestra, the Bolshoi Ballet, and the National Kabuki Theater Troupe appear at Moonbase annually. Among the professional groups that have played at Moonbase are the Royal Shakespeare Company, the Shanghai Opera, the Nova Dance Theatre of Halifax, and many others.

---

THE FIRST CONCERT ON THE MOON

On New Year's Day 2015, the first formal concert was performed on the Moon.

Moonbase and Lunagrad were still under construction, but the men and women of the two communities decided to celebrate the New Year together—one of the few holidays

---

that almost everyone on the Moon shared.

The concert was held at Moonbase, in the partly finished Main Plaza, which was the only enclosed area large enough to hold the 900 people attending. The lunar orchestra consisted entirely of Moonbase and Lunagrad workers who were amateur musicians. They brought their own instruments, although Lunagrad provided a baby grand piano that had been brought to the Soviet facility piece by piece by various Russians as part of their personal cargo allotments and then lovingly rebuilt.

The opening piece of the concert was a Beethoven piano solo, played by Lev Brudnoy, a Russian communications technician: the "Moonlight" Sonata.

Dance in one-sixth gravity is especially spectacular. Newcomers to the Moon are invariably awed at the heights a dancer can leap, and the dreamlike slowness of motion that the low gravity permits. A whole new vocabulary of dance steps is being created at Moonbase and Lunagrad.

Drama, dance, and musical offerings are staged in the Moonbase Theater, located in the Main Plaza. Performances by Moonbase personnel are usually either free or bear only a nominal charge to defray the costs of the production. Ticket prices for performances by artists from Earth, however, are based mainly on the price charged by the artists. Moonbase

Inc. generally subsidizes such performances by providing roundtrip transportation.

Athletic Activities. In an environment where the average person can high-jump more than 6 meters (over 20 feet), athletics and sports on the Moon are exciting and *different*.

Human-Powered Flight. The one sport that everyone wants to try at Moonbase is flying. In one-sixth gravity, the average human being's Earth-born muscles are sufficiently strong to provide loft and propulsion, if the person is fitted with a proper set of wings.

Lunar flying is somewhat like hang gliding, but it is perfectly possible actually to *fly*, not merely glide. Using nothing but one's own muscle power, a person can lift off the ground, climb, soar, even do aerobatics in the gentle lunar gravity.

Of course, a flier must have air in which to fly. Wings do not work in a vacuum. The only enclosed and air-filled space large enough for flying, at present, is the vault covering the Main Plaza. Since the floor area is usually crowded with shoppers, sightseers, and people on other business, all takeoffs and landings are restricted to the designated fliers' areas in the upper tiers of the vault. Fliers who "buzz" pedestrians on the main floor of the plaza will not be allowed to fly again.

The wings used for flying are made of monolayer plastic, manufactured in zero-gravity facilities at LEO, and braced with ultra-lightweight struts made of lunar magnesium. Management of all flying is the responsibility of the Tourism Program Office. Wings can be rented at the Tourism office in the Main Plaza.

Swimming. One of the most popular recreational and social areas of Moonbase is the swimming pool, located inside a moisture-proof dome at the far end of the Main Plaza. Psychological studies have shown that the availability of a swimming facility has had a strong positive effect on Moonbasers' sense of well-being and safety.

The pool is Olympic-size, with an additional area for diving at one end. Diving platforms are at 10, 20, and 30 meters height (33, 66, and 99 feet).

Water for the pool is cycled through the Moonbase system. It is not used only for the recreational facility, but is part of the base's potable water reservoir. Instead of using chlorine, the water is cleansed with abundant lunar oxygen, which is a better bactericide than chlorine and does not sting the eyes.

Court Games. Although lack of space inside Moonbase makes it impossible to conduct sporting events that require large playing fields, our residents still have a wide range of sports available to them—some organized, many not. Court games such as handball, tennis, jai alai, and volleyball are all popular.

Basketball has become a truly three-dimensional game, with the hoops placed 10 meters (nearly 33 feet) above the floor. In lunar basketball, the playing area includes the walls surrounding the court! The walls are made of transparent plastic; spectators watch from outside the court.

Football. With necessity as its mother, a new form of soccer (European football) has been invented at Moonbase. Often called *linear football*, this game is played in the base's corridors. It apparently started among a mixed group of young men and women, and has been developed rapidly by residents from the many nations where soccer is the national pastime. The Department of Health and Safety has cooperated to the extent of closing certain corridors at certain times to all traffic, so that games may be played without impediment or danger to nonplayers. However, residents (especially youngsters) often play pick-up games in the corridors without such protection. *These games are considered illegal and can be dangerous to pedestrians.* Players may be detained by security personnel and will be held responsible for any damages or injuries incurred.

---

### LINEAR FOOTBALL RULES*

1. Any number may play. There are no teams. Each individual plays as an individual.

2. Any corridor of Moonbase may serve as a playing field, if it has been so designated by Management. (Pick-up games that are not registered with Security so that the corridor is closed to ordinary traffic are strictly forbidden.)

3. The "ball" is any small object that may be kicked easily. Plastic pint containers are most often used as a "ball."

4. Goal areas are the doorways in the corridor.

5. The object of the game is to kick the ball into a goal area. Any goal area. The

---

player who scores the most goals during the game wins. Everybody else loses. There is no second place in Linear Football.

6. Each player attempts to score as many goals as possible, while preventing every other player from scoring goals.

7. Physical contact is inevitable, but should be kept below the level of general mayhem. If possible.

---

*These rules appeared anonymously in the Moonbase electronic bulletin board several years ago. No other rules for the game have ever been published.

Surface Activities. Ever since Apollo 14 astronaut Alan Shepard hit a golf ball on the Moon, in 1971, people have speculated about the possibilities of conducting sports and athletic events on the Moon's surface. Such events are discouraged both at Moonbase and Lunagrad, for two principal and interrelated reasons.

Safety is the primary consideration. The Moon's surface, with its high radiation flux, its rugged and often difficult terrain, and its high vacuum is *not* the place for fun and games. Also, fully pressurized suits are necessary for survival on the surface, and they are not well adapted for athletic activities. Pressurized suits tend to be stiff; it can be difficult to flex the arms and legs, despite the many improvements that have been made in them over the years. The thermal radiators of the suits are not considered adequate to dissipate the amounts of body heat that would be generated by intense athletic activity.

Crawler Races. There is one surface competitive activity, however, that has become an annual event at Moonbase: the cross-country crawler race, which takes place each year between Christmas and New Year's Day. Moonbase's personnel modify surface crawlers (usually spending hundreds of hours of their own time during the year) for long-duration travel at relatively high speeds. The all-time speed record in one of these races was an average of 17.7 kilometers per hour (11 mph). The annual cross-country race begins and ends at Moonbase; the far point of the race is usually across Mare Nubium at the Fra Mauro region, the crater Opelt, or a similar destination. Radiation shelters, consisting of buried habitation modules capable of supporting up to a dozen persons, are spaced at 10-kilometer (6-mile) intervals along each route in case of an unpredicted solar radiation storm.

Lunar Olympics. Each year Moonbase and Lunagrad jointly sponsor the Lunar Olympic Games. The Games, which consist mainly of track and field events, plus basketball and any special category that the joint Olympics Committee agrees upon, are open to all residents of Lunagrad and Moonbase, whether temporary or permanent. The only stipulation is that no full-time or professional athletes are allowed to compete. Like its progenitor in ancient Greece, the Lunar Olympics are for ordinary citizens, not specialized athletes.

"First Footprints." One of the most popular

forms of surface activity is simply walking across the lunar terrain. Noncompetitive and only mildly athletic, Moonwalks are allowed and even encouraged—under proper supervision.

New arrivals and tourists often seek to plant their footprints in the dusty lunar regolith, "where no man has gone before." The First Footprints Club has become an international organization, loosely organized in a manner similar to that of the Neptune's Courts that once initiated shipboard passengers who crossed the equator for the first time.

Tours. Regular tours are provided for residents and visitors alike to sites such as Tranquility Base, where astronauts Neil Armstrong and Buzz Aldrin first touched down on the Moon in their Apollo 11 craft; the Straight Wall, south of Alphonsus; the rayed crater Copernicus; and elsewhere. By far the most popular tourist attraction is Tranquility Base, where the lower half of the Apollo 11 landing craft still stands surrounded by the flag, equipment, and footprints Armstrong and Aldrin left there. The regolith has been covered with a clear plastic so that the astronauts' historic footprints cannot be disturbed.

Tours of Lunagrad are also available, although Star City, on the far side, is off-limits to tourists. This is because Star City is a working astronomical research center, where extremely sensitive radio-telescope searches of the heavens are underway, seeking possible signals from other intelligent races. Moonbase residents may visit Star City if they are recommended by one of the astronomical facility's research staff members.

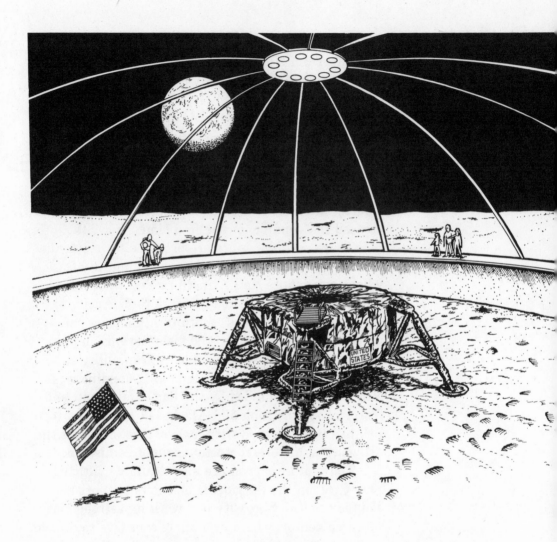

APOLLO 11 MONUMENT (Flag bent from blast-off)

Surface Safety. Moonbase residents can, of course, take walks on the surface or even join one of the tourist jaunts to historic sites such as Tranquility Base. All tours are led by personnel from the Tourism Program Office, and are subject to the regulations established by that office. Moonbase personnel may go on such tours free of charge, on a standby basis. To assure a reservation on a particular tour, however, it is necessary to purchase a tour ticket at the regular price.

Any Moonbase resident who wishes to walk on the surface must follow the regulations laid down by the Department of Health and Safety. All surface suits must be checked out by H&S personnel who are on duty at each airlock at all times. *No one is allowed to walk on the surface alone,* except in the specially marked "Moonwalk Lanes" on the floor of Alphonsus, close to the base. (See the "Lunar Tourism" chapter.)

It is possible to borrow a crawler for a longer-range excursion, provided you can produce an authorized operator's license.

All surface excursions are subject to the control of the Department of Health and Safety. Radio orders to return to Moonbase or to seek immediate shelter must be obeyed. Failure to do so can result in injury, harmful radiation exposure, even death. An employee's contract may be terminated for failure to follow Health and Safety commands.

Surface Suits. Pressure suits for lunar surface excursions are similar in many ways to the protective suits used for Extravehicular Activity (EVA) aboard spacecraft and space stations. Basically, the suits are self-contained ecologies capable of protecting a person from vacuum, radiation, and temperature extremes over a time period ranging from twelve to seventy-two hours, depending on the type of suit employed. Pressure suits maintain an adequate air pressure within them, and provide the user with oxygen, heating/cooling, water (and in some special cases, food concentrates), and a communications link. Lights, tools, and other special equipment can be carried on the outside of the suit.

There are two major differences between an EVA in space and an excursion on the lunar surface.

First, a condition of weightlessness is almost always present in space. On the Moon, a gravitational field one-sixth Earth-normal gravity prevails.

Second, in space the hard vacuum is tainted only by the outgassing of the spacecraft and/or the suit itself. On the Moon's surface, the vacuum is accompanied by dust stirred up from the regolith, and the slight but significant electromagnetic fields generated by the impact of the ionized solar wind upon the lunar surface. This can cause dust to cling electrostatically to a walking person's suit, raising the dangers of abrading the suit joints, clogging unsealed equipment, and lowering visibility through the helmet visor. All lunar suits include dust shrouds and electrostatic "wipers" to clear the helmet visor. No suit is considered complete without them, and no person should attempt to walk on the surface without this equipment.

The most widely used type of pressure suit is the so-called "hard suit." Made of rigid, lightweight metals and composite materials (except for its joints), the hard suit provides radiation meteoric-dust protection while maintaining a high degree of flexibility. Some hard suits are provided with internal servomotor systems that amplify the muscular movements of the arms or legs on demand, giving the user additional mobility.

The newer "flex suits" are still in the testing stage and are used only by selected personnel. Instead of rigid metal or composite segments, the flex suits are made entirely of soft Lunathane* plastic. One of the breakthrough discoveries made by Moonbase scientists, Lunathane remains as flexible as ordinary fabrics even when pressurized to 10 pounds per square inch in a high vacuum. It is an excellent thermal insulator and offers good protection against solar radiation.

When the current testing program is concluded, flex suits will start to replace the hard suits so widely used today.

**Worship**
Moonbase's residents, both temporary and permanent, come from every part of Earth and represent every major religion. Religious services are held regularly at the Moonbase Interfaith Chapel, in the

---

*Lunathane is a registered trade name and the property of Moonbase Inc. The composition of this plastic material is proprietary and may not be discussed with *anyone* unless specifically permitted by Moonbase's Administration Division.

Main Dome. In addition, worship services are scheduled as requested at other public areas and even in private quarters.

Moonbase's clergy provide professional services in addition to their religious duties. Many are physicians, nurses, or psychological counselors. Others are geologists, astronomers, teachers, and—in one case—an operatically trained tenor who founded and still leads Moonbase's choir and glee club.

Television transmission from Earth allows Moonbase residents to attend electronically virtually every major religious celebration, from Rome, Mecca, Jerusalem, Calcutta, Tokyo, Westminster Abbey, Salt Lake City, and elsewhere.

---

### THE FIRST RELIGIOUS CEREMONY ON THE MOON

The earliest formal religious observance on the Moon was performed by Fr. Auguste Lenoire, the French-Canadian Jesuit priest and geologist who took part in the Mason, Lenoire, and Wayne overland traverse of the Mare Imbrium region in 2006.

Father Lenoire said mass every morning, outside the ground vehicle used for the traverse, standing on the regolith in his hard suit. By the fourth day, Mason and Wayne, a Baptist and an atheist, respectively, joined their companion for the morning service.

"We grew so close," said Mason, "that we

---

couldn't stand the sight of him alone, all by himself. It didn't seem right."

"Besides," added Wayne, a self-professed atheist, "we needed all the help we could get out there."

# Hub of the Solar System: Lunar Transportation Node

Moonbase is undoubtedly the most important transportation node in the solar system. The current exploration of Mars, the development of resource centers among the Main Belt asteroids, and the probes of the other planets and moons of the solar system are all entirely dependent on lunar resources, facilities, and personnel. Lunar resources also feed the growing industrial, commercial, and scientific facilities in Earth orbit.

The key to Moonbase's importance in space transportation derives from two basic physical facts:

1. Because of the Moon's low gravity and airlessness, it takes twenty-two times less energy to launch a payload from the Moon than from the Earth. With a fully operational and nearly self-sufficient Moonbase, this means that it is very nearly twenty-two times less expensive to launch payloads from the Moon than from Earth.

Spacecraft lifting from Earth carry less than five percent of their total weight as payload. Most of their liftoff weight consists of the propellants necessary to overcome the Earth's gravity. Spacecraft lifting from the Moon can be 50 percent payload—and the unmanned cargoes launched by Moonbase's mass driver are more than 90 percent payload!

2. The Moon is rich in resources that are important to space transportation and construction. Among those resources are construction materials such as aluminum, magnesium, silicon, titanium, and steel; propellants such as oxygen and aluminum; electronic materials such as silicon and gallium; and life support supplies such as oxygen and food.

**Importance of Space Stations**

Around the turn of the century, when the first manned landings on the Moon since 1972 were being made by Russians and Americans, the two nations' space stations in low Earth orbit (LEO) were vital transportation nodes. Here the lunarbound vehicles were assembled from components lifted from Earth. Here they were fueled by Earth-based tankers and stocked with supplies. The lunar crews checked out their spacecraft at the space stations.

When crews returned from the Moon their spacecraft were checked out, refurbished, and stored at the space stations until ready for use again. Propellants and supplies were also stored at the LEO stations.

By far the largest tonnage of all the materials lifted from Earth was oxygen, in its liquified cryogenic form. Liquid oxygen was (and still is) used for life support, for the fuel cells that generate electricity aboard spacecraft, but mainly as a rocket propellant. Rocket engines must carry an oxidizer in which their fuel can be burned, since there is no air in space for them to "breathe." Indeed, most of the mass of spacecraft leaving LEO and heading for the Moon consisted of liquid hydrogen and liquid oxygen (rocket fuel and oxidizer, respectively). For example, a lunar landing vehicle that delivered thirty tons of payload to the Moon's surface required nearly two hundred tons of propellant!

Moreover, most of the propellant mass was oxygen. The ratio of oxygen to hydrogen was always at least six to one, by mass. Thus approximately 75 percent of *all* the mass lifted from Earth was oxygen.

Clearly, if lunar oxygen could replace oxygen lifted from Earth, it would result in a great cost saving.

---

CRYOGENICS

The science of cryogenics deals with extremely low temperatures. When rocket propellants such as hydrogen and oxygen are liquified from their usual gaseous state they are said to be cryogenic propellants.

Rocket propellants are liquified to reduce the size of the spacecraft tankage; when cooled down to the point where they liquify, gases such as hydrogen and oxygen are reduced in volume by a factor of more than 800, which means they can be carried in much smaller tanks. This saves structural weight in the spacecraft and boosters, as well as allowing them to be designed more compactly.

Hydrogen liquifies at a temperature of $-252.8°$ C ($-423°$ F); oxygen at $-183°$ C ($-297°$ F).

---

**The Oxygen Trade** This is why one of the first "temporary" camps set up on the Moon was quickly developed into a highly automated facility for producing liquified oxygen out of lunar regolith materials. This earliest "Lunox*" facility was built to operate unattended for months at a time. It produced 150 tons of liquid oxygen per

---

*Lunox is a registered trade name of Moonbase Inc. and as such should always be capitalized.

month. It changed forever the way the human race operates in space.

Until the Lunox facility went "on line," all space missions depended entirely on propellants and supplies from Earth. In effect, this was a tether, a leash—and a very short one, at that—that kept all space missions tied closely to Earth. In those primitive days, space missions were actually "sorties," brief flights into orbit or to the Moon. Permanent occupation of space by human beings was not economically possible.

To be sure, there were several space stations in LEO, and probes had been sent out to explore the other planets of the solar system. But the space stations were small and expensive to maintain. They could not be expanded into the huge orbiting facilities we have today as long as they were dependent on Earth for every molecule of oxygen and all the other supplies they required. The planetary probes were remotely controlled unmanned vehicles that provided enormous new scientific information about the other worlds of our solar system, but also raised fascinating new questions that could be answered only by human explorers. Yet manned planetary missions that required many months or even years in transit were beyond the capabilities of turn-of-the-century space technology, for economic reasons as much as technological ones.

The availability of lunar oxygen was the first step in breaking that short tether, the first step toward giving the human race the freedom to expand throughout the solar system.

The step was not taken cheaply. More than four hundred tons of equipment had to be landed on the Moon before the Lunox facility could go into operation. More than sixty lunar landing missions were required, over a period of three and a half years. Five lives were lost.

What developed, though, was a trade between the space stations in LEO and the growing Lunox facility on the Moon—the facility that became the seed from which Moonbase grew.

Moonbound spacecraft left the space stations carrying cargos of hydrogen (in addition to other payloads such as equipment, supplies, and personnel). They delivered the hydrogen to the Lunox facility, where it was used partly to produce water and partly for the chemical process that yielded oxygen from the powdery topmost layer of the regolith, the sandy material that the geologists call "fines." The spacecraft left the Moon and headed back to LEO loaded with lunar oxygen.

In effect, lunar oxygen became a commodity that was traded for whatever the early lunar bases required. The spacecraft that returned to the space stations in LEO carried enough Lunox to repay the costs of their trip to the Moon, plus a "profit" of lunar oxygen that could be delivered to the factories and other facilities that were being built in LEO at that time.

**The Lunox Facility**      The original Lunox facility used a process in which hydrogen was reacted with ilmenite from the lunar regolith to produce water. Some of the water was stored for life support and housekeeping at the Lunox facility. A smaller percentage was shipped to other lunar bases, for similar purposes. More than 90 percent of the water, however, was electrolyzed into its component gases, hydrogen and oxygen. The hydrogen was kept at the Lunox facility for further use in the process. The oxygen was shipped Earthward.

Thus, once the Lunox facility became operational, it was able to provide a significant share of its own hydrogen input, cutting the amount that had to be imported from Earth to the small quantity required to make up losses. As the facility improved in efficiency and grew in size, proportionately less and less imported hydrogen was needed.

The powdery lunar soil was scraped from the regolith by automated front-end loaders that carried the undifferentiated fines to a shaker screen. There the larger rocks were separated, and the finer powder was carried by conveyor belt to a two-stage separator. Using standard electrostatic techniques long established in ore-processing plants on Earth, the separator removed the oxygen-bearing ilmenite from the rest of the soil material.

The unused material, which consisted of more than 90 percent of the total amount of soil processed, was moved by conveyor to a dump site. It did not remain there for long, however. Much of it was used as shielding material, spread over habitation and work modules that were partially buried in trenches, to protect their interiors against radiation and micrometeorites.

The separated ilmenite was fed into a hydrogen reduction unit where it was heated to 700° C (1,292° F) at a pressure of 2.7 atmospheres (1 atmosphere equals 14.7 pounds per square inch, or 1.033 kilograms per square centimeter). Under these conditions, approximately 10 percent of the ilmenite mass was extracted as oxygen, combined with the hydrogen in the form of water vapor. The hydrogen combines chemically with the iron oxide in the ilmenite ($FeO . TiO_2$) in accordance with the formula:

$$H_2 + FeO.TiO_2 + HEAT \rightarrow Fe + TiO_2 + H_2O$$

The powdered iron (Fe) and titanium oxide ($TiO_2$) produced in this process were then stockpiled for future use as construction materials.

The water vapor was then cooled by a radiator system until it became liquid. At that point the water was separated into two batches: one for use in the lunar bases, the other for electrolysis. The amount retained for lunar use varied depending on the needs of the moment, but at all times the Lunox facility managers sought to keep it below the 10 percent mark.

Electrical energy was applied to the water, splitting it into gaseous hydrogen and oxygen.

$$2H_2O + ENERGY \rightarrow 2H_2 + O_2$$

The hydrogen was reapplied to the input of the processing operation. The oxygen was liquified and stored in well-insulated tanks in readiness for export.

The electrolysis and liquification units both generated large amounts of heat. In the vacuum of the

Moon's surface, the surest way to get rid of unwanted heat was through radiation. Convection and conduction, two of the most common ways to dispose of excess heat on Earth, do not work in a vacuum. (Although it is possible, on the Moon, to conduct heat into the lunar soil. In effect, the solid body of the Moon becomes a "sink" for unwanted heat.)

Thus the electrolysis and liquification units were equipped with large radiator surfaces. Some of the heat generated in these processes was eventually routed through heat exchangers and used to preheat the incoming ore in preparation for separation and oxygen removal.

To produce a nominal 150 tons of oxygen per month, the Lunox facility required an electrical power capacity of 6,000 kilowatts. This was provided by a nuclear power plant. By far the heaviest piece of equipment brought to the Moon at that time, the power plant massed more than 200 tons. It is still in use, mainly as a back-up facility for Moonbase's solarvoltaic energy farms.

In those bootstrap years, the Lunox facility not only supplied oxygen as an "export item" to pay for "importing" equipment and supplies; some of the oxygen and water produced at the Alphonsus base was used by the Moon-based team themselves for life support and transportation.

The oxygen-production facilities were constantly upgraded. Among the first steps toward improving the efficiency of the system was to use heat from sunlight, focused by parabolic mirrors, to preheat the ilmenite and to dissociate the water directly, eliminating the need for electrolysis. This, combined with the growing amount of electrical energy provided by solarvoltaic cells, allowed Moonbase to convert the original nuclear power plant to its current back-up role.

Today, *all* the oxygen used off-Earth comes from the Moon, except for the oxygen generated on the moons and surface of Mars by the exploration teams based there.

And today, of course, oxygen is processed from lunar ores by a variety of means, including the original hydrogen reduction process. Most of the latest techniques for oxygen production are the proprietary techniques of Moonbase Inc., and are not for public discussion. If you are going to be employed in the oxygen production facilities of the Transportation Program Office, you will be expected to maintain secrecy concerning corporate proprietary information.

**Expanding Trade**

From exporting oxygen, it was a relatively easy step to export rocket fuels and construction materials, as well.

Powdered aluminum was the first rocket fuel exported from the Moon. At first the aluminum was produced by scavenging spent rocket stages. Instead of leaving the empty tankage and spacecraft shells on the lunar surface, they were processed into powdered aluminum and used to fuel lunar hoppers and lobbers. Tankage left in orbit around the Moon was also recovered and used.

Aluminum fuel is not as efficient as hydrogen for

rocket propulsion. Rocket efficiency is rated in terms of specific impulse, essentially a measure of how many seconds a gram of propellants will produce a gram of thrust. For various fuel-oxidizer mixtures, specific impulse ($I^{SP}$) is rated as follows:

| Fuel | Oxidizer | Specific Impulse |
| --- | --- | --- |
| Hydrogen | Oxygen | 460–485 sec |
| Silane | Oxygen | 370–400 sec |
| Al/HTPB | Oxygen | 290–310 sec |
| Aluminum | Oxygen | 270 sec |

Silane is a compound of silicon and hydrogen ($SiH_4$); silicon is abundant on the Moon, but the hydrogen must be imported from Earth.

Al/HTPB is a mixture of aluminum and a solid-rocket propellant, hydroxyterminated polybutadine, similar to the kind used in the strap-on solid-rocket motors for the original space shuttle. The aluminum is easily available on the Moon, but the HTPB must be imported.

Although the aluminum/oxygen propulsion system is not as efficient as the others, it has the great advantage of using only lunar resources. There is no need for any material to be brought up from Earth.

Lunar oxygen can also be used as the sole propellant in rocket systems where the basic energy is derived from nuclear heat or electricity, rather than from chemical combustion.

In a nuclear-powered spacecraft, the heat generated by a nuclear reaction is used to accelerate a "working fluid," or propellant. The lighter the molecular weight of the propellant, the more velocity it will gain from the same input of heat. Thus the most efficient nuclear-powered spacecraft utilize hydrogen as their propellant. Nuclear-powered spacecraft that use lunar oxygen propellant have relatively low specific impulses, up to 120 sec.

Lunar oxygen (as well as other propellants) can be used in conjunction with an electrical rocket system, such as an ion thruster or a plasma arc jet. Although very high specific impulses are obtained, in the range of 3,000 to 10,000 sec, electrical propulsion systems generally produce very low thrusts. This is because the system must carry an on-board electrical power generator, and the more thrust desired, the larger the generator must be.

Low-thrust systems cannot attain high velocities quickly. But because electrical rockets are very efficient, they can continue to operate for extremely long periods of time. Picture a bicyclist in a race against a sports car. The sports car can easily out-accelerate the cyclist and can go much faster—until it runs out of fuel. The cyclist can eventually pedal past the stranded sports car and keep on going indefinitely (as long as the cyclist can eat while pedaling).

Low-thrust electrical rockets, therefore, are used for unmanned cargo missions between LEO and lunar orbit, and for very-long-duration missions, such as unmanned probes to the distant planets. For missions that go as far as the Main Asteroid Belt, some 400 million kilometers (250 million miles) from the Sun, solar cells can provide the electricity for the electrical rockets. At distances beyond that, nuclear power sources are used.

Lunar oxygen is one of the major propellants used in electrical rockets throughout the solar system. Again, propellants with lighter molecular weights, such as hydrogen, helium, lithium, and nitrogen, offer higher specific impulses. but lunar oxygen is abundant and inexpensive, two factors that work in its favor in almost every space mission.

A competing low-thrust, high-efficiency form of space transportation is the solar sail. Huge gossamer sails of ultrathin plastic, several square kilometers in area, catch the microscopic pressure of sunlight and glide through the frictionless vacuum of interplanetary space. Of the fifteen solar sail automated probes now drifting outward toward the fringes of the solar system, exploring the Main Asteroid Belt, the gas giant planets and their moons, and the interplanetary plasma, eight are "powered" by sails made at Moonbase, and six were built entirely by Moonbase.

**The Mass Driver**

The most efficient form of transportation at Moonbase does not use rockets of any kind. It is the railgun, or mass driver, a form of electrical catapult.

The mass driver is used for lifting cargo off the lunar surface, mainly shipments of ore, oxygen, and refined metals that are used in the manufacturing facilities and space stations at LEO.

The English futuristic author Arthur C. Clarke first suggested that electrical catapults might be used on the Moon, nearly a century ago. By the 1970s, researchers such as Gerard K. O'Neill of

Princeton University were developing the technology of mass drivers, and by the turn of the century work done at the University of Texas had produced a practical railgun system.

The Moonbase mass driver is located on Mare Nubium, approximately 30 kilometers (less than 19 miles) from the outer rim of Alphonsus.

The mass driver is essentially a linear synchronous motor, a kind of electric motor that is laid out in a straight line. Electrical energy is used to accelerate the cargo-carrying "buckets" to lunar orbital velocity: 1.6 km/sec (0.99 mi/sec). By comparison, Earth's orbital velocity is 7.9 km/sec (4.9 mi/sec). In addition to the lower orbital velocity, the Moon's lack of atmosphere means that there is no air friction to hinder the catapult launches.

If the energy required to boost a payload is expressed in terms of kilowatt-hours, then it takes approximately 11,000 kilowatt-hours of energy to lift a ton of payload from Earth's surface into LEO. To lift a ton of payload from the Moon's surface to escape velocity requires only 800 kilowatt-hours. In addition, Earth's thick blanket of atmosphere causes drag that must be overcome by further expenditure of energy, while the Moon is airless. The result is that payloads can be launched from the Moon to LEO twenty-two times more cheaply than lifting them from the Earth to LEO.

The mass driver is 3.5 kilometers (2.17 miles) long. The cargo carriers are levitated along its track by powerful magnetic fields and accelerated at more than 100 *g*. That is more than 100 times the Earth's gravitational force. By comparison, rockets launched from the Earth pull no more than 3 to 4 *g*. Clearly, the mass driver is *not* used for launching people!

The magnets used in the mass driver are *superconducting*. They are composed of alloys of metals, oxygen, and rare earth elements. Although many of these materials are available on the Moon, the magnets were manufactured on Earth completely from terrestrial materials and transported to Moonbase in 150-ton segments. The entire mass-driver facility totals 20,000 tons.

When kept properly cooled, superconductors lose all resistance to electrical current, and thus can run at full power with no need for electricity, once energized. They do require liquid nitrogen, however, to maintain their low temperature. Although it is much easier to maintain cryogenic temperatures on the Moon's surface than on Earth (vacuum is an excellent insulator), some nitrogen is lost over the course of a year's operation and must be made up by importation from Earth.

A second mass driver is now under construction, using a new type of "room temperature" superconducting magnets that do not require cryogenic cooling. These magnets—as well as all the other components of the new mass driver—are being constructed entirely from lunar materials.

The mass driver regularly launches between five and six million tons of material each year to the facilities in LEO, at a cost of less than US $10 per ton.

The cargos launched by the mass driver are collected by the mass catcher in high lunar polar orbit, and from there are shipped to LEO by nuclear-powered freight carriers.

Originally it was planned to place the mass catcher at the L2 libration point, above the Moon's far side. But because of the extremely sensitive radiotelescope searches for extraterrestrial signals being conducted at Star City, the mass catcher has been established in a high polar orbit that circles the Moon in slightly more than two and a half days at an altitude of 50,000 kilometers (about 31,000 miles).

## Crossroads of Space

As lunar propellants, construction materials, and ores became more and more important to space industries and exploration, Moonbase—with its L1 space station—has become the nexus for the vast majority of space missions.

The LEO space stations are still an important first staging area for personnel from Earth who are going into space. But today most of the propellants and construction material for space missions come from Moonbase and its associated mining and manufacturing centers. Most of the spacecraft for missions to Mars, the Asteroid Belt, and beyond are actually constructed at the L1 station.

Thanks to its strategic position and its natural resources, the Moon has become literally the hub of the solar system.

The continuing exploration of the planet Mars is supplied from Moonbase. Outward-bound Mars spacecraft are assembled and checked out at L1. Returning Mars spacecraft come to L1 for repair and refurbishment.

The growing stream of prospecting vehicles heading for the Main Asteroid Belt, between Mars and Jupiter, are built at the L1 facility from metals and plastics manufactured at Moonbase. Increasingly, their electronic systems are manufactured at Moonbase, as well. Naturally, their propellants and life support supplies are provided by Moonbase. Of the eight Belt spacecraft launched in the past two years, only the nuclear reactors have been built on Earth; Moonbase supplied all the other components, equipment, and supplies.

The Solar Power Satellites, which beam energy to the Earth from geosynchronous Earth orbit (GEO), were built almost entirely from lunar materials. Moonbase Inc. is currently negotiating with the governments of Japan, India, and Brazil for construction of three new 10,000-megawatt Solar Power Satellites.

**Asteroid Mining**

Asteroids are minor planets. The largest of them, Ceres, is roughly 800 kilometers (500 miles) in diameter. Asteroids down to diameters of approximately one kilometer have been observed from the Moon. More than 100,000 asteroids have been detected in the Main Belt, and their orbits calculated.

The Main Belt asteroids are an incredibly rich source of metals and minerals. Although they lie beyond the orbit of Mars, the Main Belt asteroids contain the heavy metals and volatiles that the Moon does not.

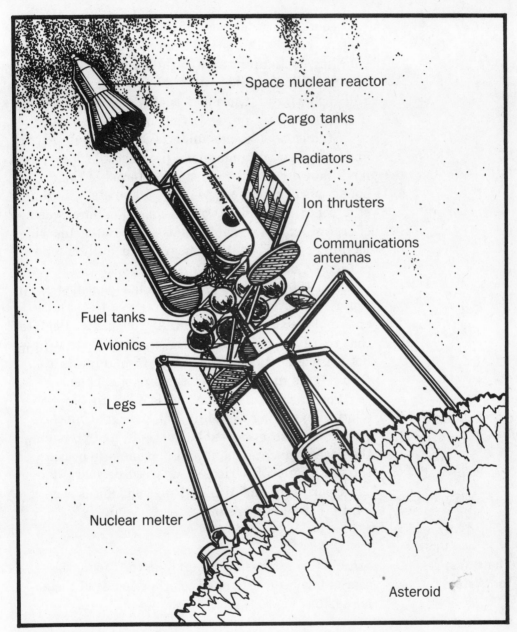

Space nuclear reactor

Cargo tanks

Radiators

Ion thrusters

Communications antennas

Fuel tanks

Avionics

Legs

Nuclear melter

Asteroid

ROBOT ASTEROID MINER

About ninety percent of them are of the stony variety, relatively low in heavy metals but rich in volatiles, including water in the form of hydrates. The metallic asteroids, although fewer in number, still represent an enormous supply of iron, nickel, chromium, platinum, and other precious metals.

Studies of asteroids undertaken with automated and teleoperated unmanned "prospector" spacecraft have shown that a single stony asteroid of the carbonaceous chondritic type, some 100 meters in diameter, contains hundreds of millions of dollars' worth of organic chemicals and volatiles. A 100-meter-wide metallic asteroid contains nearly four million tons of high-grade nickel steel.

The 100,000 Main Belt asteroids identified so far represent more metal and mineral wealth than the entire planet Earth can yield. Astronomers calculate that there are trillions of smaller asteroids that have not yet been catalogued, ranging from a few hundred meters in diameter to the size of pebbles.

For this reason, Moonbase is devoting a major effort to exploring the Main Belt, designating the richest and most accessible asteroids, and preparing the necessary equipment and personnel to operate in the Main Belt for periods of up to three years. The Transportation and Mining Program Offices are jointly managing this effort.

**The Quest for Water**

Since no water has been found on the Moon, the search has been expanded to other bodies of the solar system.

The planet Mars has extensive polar caps of frozen water. Martian exploration teams use this resource for life support on the planet's surface. However, the energy required to land on the surface of Mars is more than double the energy required for landing on the Moon. (Mars's escape velocity is 5.03 km/sec; the Moon's 2.38.) Once on the surface, the spacecraft must then take off again. The economics dictated by these energy requirements makes importing water from Mars very nearly as expensive as importing water from Earth.

Mars's two small moons, Deimos and Phobos, however, are relatively rich in water. They apparently were once free-roaming asteroids that fell into Mars's gravitational "well" and were trapped into orbiting the planet. Detailed studies have shown that the moons are similar in composition to the carbonaceous chondritic asteroids. More than 15 percent of their total masses consist of water, chemically locked to the rocks in the form of hydrates. This amounts to $10^{15}$ tons—a million billion tons—of water!

Because the Martian moons are so small (Phobos is 28 kilometers long, Deimos 16), their gravitational fields are negligible. Escape velocities are 0.016 and 0.008 km/sec, respectively. Therefore it would be much cheaper, in terms of energy and economics, to "mine" water from Phobos and Deimos than any other source yet found in the solar system.

However, the International Astronautical Authority has not permitted any economic or industrial utilization of the planet Mars or its satellites. Despite repeated appeals by Moonbase Inc., several of the governments that are principal shareholders in Moonbase, and the government of the Soviet Union (on behalf of Lunagrad), the IAA has maintained the position that *no* utilization of Mars or its moons may be permitted until the current scientific exploration of the planet definitely establishes whether or not living forms exist or have existed on Mars.

Consequently, Moonbase is considering two other possible sources of extraterrestrial water: asteroids and comets.

Asteroids. While most of the asteroids are in the Main Belt between Mars and Jupiter, nearly one hundred asteroids follow orbits that take them much closer to the Sun and across the orbit of Earth. The *Apollo* group of asteroids all cross the Earth's orbit. A smaller group, the *Atens*, orbit between the Earth and the Sun. The *Amor* group are farther out and cross the orbits of both Mars and Earth. These bodies are called near-Earth asteroids (NEAs).

Automated and later manned missions to the twenty nearest NEAs have shown that three of them are carbonaceous chondrites and contain between 15 percent and 20 percent water, in the form of hydrates. Although the IAA has prohibited all activities on NEAs except basic research, Moonbase Inc. expects this ban to be lifted on at least one NEA within the coming year. At that time, manned operations on asteroid 2100 Ra-Shalom will begin the process of water extraction on an experimental basis. All other NEAs will remain off-limits to all operations except research.

Comets. Long described as "dirty snowballs,"

comets are bodies of frozen volatiles such as water, oxygen, nitrogen, etc., in which are mixed stones of various sizes. Most comets come close enough to the Sun to be seen from Earth and the Moon only once, then swing out on parabolic orbits that carry them away from the solar system forever. Other comets have less eccentric orbits and return to the Earth–Moon vicinity regularly. The most famous periodic comet is Halley's, which is due to return to the inner solar system during 2061–62.

Dozens of other comets return close to the Sun regularly, in periods far shorter than Halley's. Since 1985, when the first spacecraft investigation of Comet Giacobini-Zinner was made, it has been evident that comets contain abundant amounts of water and other volatiles that are relatively lacking or altogether absent on the Moon.

Halley's Comet, for example, spewed more than 30 million tons of water vapor into space during the six months of its approach to the Sun in 1985–86. While it was closest to the Sun, the comet lost an average of three tons of water per second. Halley's twelve-mile-long nucleus of dust and ice shrank by some 6 to 9 meters (20 to 30 feet) during its last visit to the inner solar system. Even at that rate of loss, it still contains enough ice for thousands of more orbits.

However, the comets that return to the Earth–Moon vicinity regularly rarely come closer than a few tens of millions of kilometers. Moreover, they are traveling at relatively high speeds in orbits of high inclination, rather than orbits that lie nearly parallel to the Earth–Moon orbital path. This means that reaching them requires considerable expenditures of energy, rocket propellants, and money.

## PERIODICAL COMETS

| Comet Name | Period (Years) | Orbital Inclination |
|---|---|---|
| Enke | 3.3 | 12.0 |
| Grigg-Skjellerup | 5.1 | 21.1 |
| Tempel 2 | 5.3 | 12.5 |
| Honda-Mrkos-Pajdusakova | 5.3 | 13.1 |
| Neujmin 2 | 5.4 | 10.6 |
| Tempel 1 | 5.5 | 10.5 |
| Tuttle-Giacobini-Kresak | 5.6 | 13.6 |
| Tempel-Swift | 5.7 | 5.4 |
| Wirtanen | 5.9 | 12.3 |
| D'Arrest | 6.2 | 16.7 |
| DuToit-Neujmin-Delporte | 6.3 | 2.9 |
| DiVico-Swift | 6.3 | 3.6 |
| Pons-Winnecke | 6.3 | 22.3 |
| Forbes | 6.4 | 4.6 |
| Kopff | 6.4 | 4.7 |
| Schwassmann-Wachmann 2 | 6.5 | 3.7 |
| Giacobini-Zinner | 6.5 | 31.7 |
| Halley | 76.1 | 64.2 |

(*Note*: Comets are named after their discoverers; except for Halley's, which is named after the English astronomer who first calculated that it returns to Earth's vicinity regularly. Frequently more than one person has discovered a comet at the same time; thus many comets have multiple names.)

Moonbase has constructed and begun to operate an unmanned, highly automated, teleoperated "scooper" vehicle that plies the inner solar system and maneuvers itself into the streaming tails of periodical comets whose orbits are of relatively low inclination. These tails are so tenuous that they are blown by the solar wind away from the Sun no matter which direction the comet is moving. They consist of gases and dust boiled off the comet's main body as it nears the Sun.

The scooper spacecraft, as its name implies, gathers up some of the cometary tail gases by use of an elongated magnetic field shaped like a funnel. The magnetic field is carried by the thin rigid wires, which are possible only in the near-zero gravitationalconditions of interplanetary space and the very low accelerations of the spacecraft's electrical propulsion system.

The lightest gases (hydrogen and helium) are used as propellants for the spacecraft's nuclear-powered electrical thrusters. Oxygen, nitrogen, and compound gases such as water, ammonia ($NH_3$), and methane ($CH_4$) are separated and stored in tanks aboard the scooper craft. Transfer tankers are sent out to the scooper when it is at its closest approach to the Moon, and take on the accumulated riches gathered from the cometary tails.

At that time, the scooper craft is refurbished, any necessary repairs are made, and new scientific instrumentation is installed for the continuing study of comets, the Sun, and the interplanetary medium.

The scooper spacecraft can also be programmed

to intercept Sun-grazing comets which enter the inner solar system only once. Some grazers do not survive their close encounter with the Sun; they are completely boiled away or, on rare occasions, actually crash into the Sun itself.

Scooper spacecraft are still operated on an experimental basis. The amounts of water and volatiles that they have provided for Moonbase are small, but well within the expected parameters of these early test flights. Within five years, scooper spacecraft

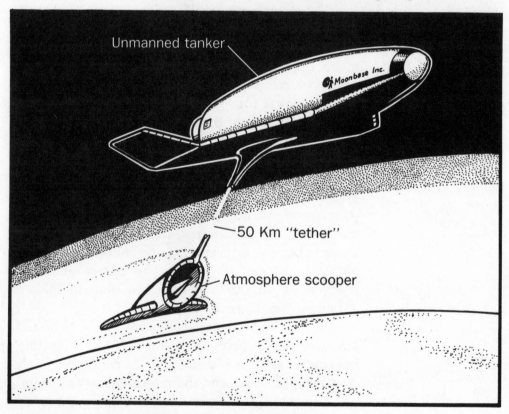

PLANETARY ATMOSPHERE "SCOOPER" CRAFT

should be able to provide Moonbase's entire current requirement for water and volatiles.

**The Quest for Intelligent Life**

Although there is a vigorous biochemistry underway beneath the clouds of Jupiter, to date no trace of extraterrestrial intelligent life has been found in the solar system. The radio searches of the sky being conducted at Star City have detected some faint signals that are possibly the work of an intelligent species, but this conclusion has not yet been confirmed.

Moonbase is working with a consortium of universities and government agencies on Earth to construct the first interstellar probe spacecraft. Unmanned, fully automated, and under the guidance of the latest artificial intelligence (AI) computer systems, the three probes now under construction will be sent to Alpha Centauri, Barnard's Star, and Wolf 359, the three stars closest to our solar system. Planets have been observed orbiting around Barnard's Star and Wolf 359. One-way trip times are expected to be between fifty and seventy-five years.

Much of the propulsion and electronics technology for these first star probes has been developed at Moonbase. The magnetic scoops that the star craft will use to gather interstellar hydrogen to fuel their fusion engines are based on the scoops developed for Moonbase's comet scooper spacecraft. The AI systems are refinements of the decision-making, self-repairing systems developed over two decades of lunar surface and space operations.

These automated probes to the stars will undoubtedly be followed by human explorers one day.

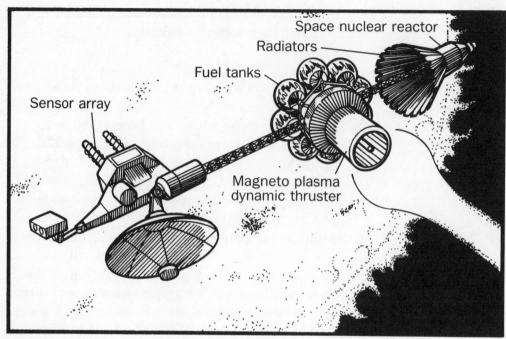

Space nuclear reactor

Radiators

Fuel tanks

Sensor array

Magneto plasma dynamic thruster

STAR PROBE

When that time comes, the star ships will be built at Moonbase, and their crews will include many of Moonbase's finest men and women.

**Future Developments**

In addition to routine transportation operations, the Transportation Program Office has given top priority to developing the cometary scooper spacecraft and Main Asteroid Belt prospector vehicles, because of their importance to Moonbase's self-sufficiency. The star probes are second in importance only to these efforts.

Scientific experiments undertaken by the Exploration and Research Program Office have shown that hypercharge, apparently a fifth universal force, may exist and may be utilized to neutralize or even reverse the effects of gravity. If this become feasible, space transportation will enter an entirely new era. (For more information on hypercharge studies, see the "Exploration and Research" chapter, p. 160)

**Career Growth Opportunities**

If your position is in the Space Transportation Program Office, you are probably an engineer or technician with a degree in astronautics, spacecraft design, rocket propulsion, electronics, life support, logistics, teleoperation, computers, or Artificial Intelligence.

In addition to upgrading your education and/or skill level, you can enhance your career by cross-training. For example, specialists in rocket propulsion work closely with specialists in spacecraft design, electronics, and logistics.

The Space Transportation Program Office also works with the oxygen production, electronics manufacturing, and spacecraft components manufacturing sections of the Mining and Manufacturing Program Office, as well as many groups in the Exploration and Research Program Office. Cross-training with personnel in those areas will increase your knowledge and skills, and make you a more valuable member of the Moonbase team.

It is also possible to work toward advanced degrees in areas that interest you, so that you can be better qualified for promotion within your specialty or transfer from your existing specialty to a different one, if you so desire.

# Moonrocks and Diamonds: Lunar Manufacturing

When men and women first returned to the Moon, around the turn of the century, hardly anyone thought that the Moon would become a major manufacturing center. Yet that is exactly what has happened.

It was expected that lunar oxygen would play an important role in the economics of space transportation. And so it has. But other lunar resources, including the resourcefulness of our people, have allowed Moonbase to develop a unique and highly profitable manufacturing capability.

The Moon has three significant advantages for manufacturing:

1. *Natural Resources.* Oxygen, silicon, aluminum, iron, titanium, calcium, and magnesium are all abundant on the Moon. For the most part, they are available on the lunar surface, as part of the regolith or in rocks ejected from meteorite impact craters and/or volcanoes. There is hardly any need to dig deep into the Moon's crust, as most mines are dug on Earth.

Lunar mining usually consists of a set of automated or teleoperated front-end loaders, which scrape the top few meters from the regolith. The rocks and powdery soil, which the mining engineers call *fines*, are loaded on carts that are towed to the refineries by crawlers.

2. *Low Gravity.* The Moon's low gravity has two beneficial effects. First, it allows lunar raw materials to be lifted off the Moon and sent to factories in LEO or elsewhere very cheaply. It takes only 800 kilowatt-hours of energy to lift a ton off the Moon. In

fact, since that is the amount of energy required to accelerate the payload to escape velocity, the energy actually expended by Moonbase's mass driver is slightly less, because payloads are sent to the mass catcher in orbit 50,000 kilometers (31,000 miles) above the Moon's poles. However, transfer spacecraft must expend energy to move the payloads from lunar orbit to LEO, so the figure of 800 kilowatt-hours per ton is reasonably accurate.

To put this expenditure of energy in terms that anyone can understand, especially anyone who has been on a diet, it takes 680 million calories to lift a ton from the Moon to escape velocity, while it takes nearly 10 *billion* calories to lift a ton from Earth to LEO.

Low gravity affects the economics of any operation that involves lifting or transporting materials from one place to another. "Trucking" on the Moon is much less expensive than terrestrial hauling; lifting requires only one-sixth the work it does on Earth.

Low gravity is important not only for the economics of transportation, but in manufacturing as well. Structures do not have to built as massively on the Moon. Delicate work, such as thin films and large pieces of glass, can be manufactured to precise tolerances without being warped, bent, or cracked by the strain of gravity. The 1,000-centimeter optical telescope mirror at the Star City observatory was manufactured on the Moon mainly because it could not have been made on Earth.

3. *High Vacuum.* While the Moon's airlessness

poses problems for life support, it is a very valuable commodity for manufacturing processes.

On Earth, factories and research laboratories spend a great deal of time, energy, and money to produce nothing—a vacuum. On the Moon, vacuum is everywhere, for free.

The unit of measurement for vacuum is the torr, named after Evangelista Torricelli, the student of Galileo who first measured air pressure and invented the barometer. On Earth, standard air pressure at sea level is 760 torr.

Vacuum has many industrial applications. On Earth, vacuums of a ten-thousandth of a torr ($10^{-4}$ torr) are used in metallurgical processes such as casting, sintering, heat treatment, and brazing. The pharmaceutical and food industries also use such vacuums to freeze-dry medicines, antibiotics, blood plasma, and foodstuffs. Vacuum down to a millionth ($10^{-6}$) of a torr is used for insulating cryogenic liquids at temperatures close to absolute zero ($-273.2°$ C, $-459.76°$ F), electrical insulation, vacuum tubes, thin-film coatings, and electron welding.

Research applications of vacuums down to $10^{-9}$ torr include electron microscopes, particle accelerators, microwave tubes, field ion microscopes, and thermonuclear fusion reactors.

It is possible to produce on Earth a vacuum as low as $10^{-11}$ torr (a hundred-billionth of a torr). To do so, however, takes special equipment and many hours of pumping work. The vacuum chamber is usually quite small, with a volume of only a few cubic meters, at most. The vacuum is ten times better,

$10^{-12}$ torr, over the entire expanse of the lunar surface—an area of some 38 million square kilometers
(nearly equal to the land area of North, Central, and
South America combined!).

Since the advantages of low gravity and vacuum
are also available at LEO (plus the availability of
near-zero gravity) most planners originally felt that
the Moon would be used mainly as a source of raw
materials, while factories and industrial facilities
would be built in orbit close to the Earth. That was
before Moonbase was started. Today, Moonbase is
not merely a "mining town"; it is a prime industrial
center.

**The Economic
Imperatives**

The first "mining" operations carried out on the
Moon were simply scooping up the topmost layers of
the regolith and covering the habitation modules of
the earliest camps with the rubble. A thickness of 2
meters (6.56 feet) was considered necessary to protect
the living and working spaces from solar radiation.

Since lunar oxygen was a key to the economic
viability of Moonbase, the first Lunox facility was
put into operation by 2005, although it did not attain
its full production capacity until more than a year
later.

Even before Moonbase was started, however,
studies had shown that it should be possible to use
native lunar materials for construction on the Moon,
and even for export to space stations and factories in
LEO. In addition to oxygen for life support and
rocket propellant, lunar metals could be used for con-

struction of new facilities and spacecraft in orbit,
and raw lunar ores could provide radiation shielding
for manned space stations in GEO, where the outer
Van Allen Belt's radiation fluxes are hazardous.

More important in those early days though, was
the use of native lunar materials in building Moonbase itself. During the bootstrap years, every gram
of native materials that could be used meant a gram
that did not have to be imported from Earth. This
had a direct and very powerful influence on the economics of Moonbase and the growth of its facilities.

As in all other aspects of Moonbase's operations,
the goal of our Mining and Manufacturing Program
Office is self-sufficiency. Today, Moonbase manufac-
tures all its own glass, metal, and concrete building

materials, including fiberglass products, together with virtually all the optical, electronic, and mechanical equipment for our research and manufacturing centers. In addition, the L1 space station has become a major manufacturer of spacecraft for deep-space missions. The prospecting vehicles now exploring the Main Asteroid Belt, the unmanned spacecraft studying the outer gas giant planets, and the three star probes were all constructed at the L1 facility almost entirely from lunar raw materials.

Moreover, Moonbase exports a variety of manufactured products to LEO and directly to Earth itself, including refined ultrapure metals and alloys, fiberglass and metal honeycomb insulation materials, electronics components assemblies, ceramics, plastics, construction materials, and a small but growing trade in lunar diamonds and other gemstones.

**Phased Growth**

Moonbase's manufacturing capabilities have grown in planned phases. Starting with the first Lunox plant, the steps included:

• Oxygen for life support and propulsion everywhere from LEO to the deepest space probes. Since 2017 all oxygen for space missions has been provided by Moonbase, except for the oxygen produced by the Mars exploration teams from local Martian resources.

• Producing glasses, crystals, glass fibers, and optical quality glass for research applications.

• Refining lunar ores to produce metal products, especially various types of steel for construction, as well as titanium and aluminum, both in ultrapure forms and in alloys, and honeycomb "sandwich" materials for insulation and structural applications.

• Developing the capability to manufacture high-quality electronics components, using lunar raw materials such as silicon and, later, relatively exotic elements such as gallium.

In each phase, the first purpose of developing the capability was to help build Moonbase itself, while the purpose of exporting raw ores, refined or processed materials, or finished products was a close second.

While many critics on Earth argued that Moonbase should serve only as a source of raw materials, which should be shipped to LEO facilities for refining and manufacturing, Moonbase Inc.'s management decided very early that finished manufactured goods cost less to ship and would bring higher prices at the markets in LEO and on Earth. Thus the drive to build up a manufacturing capability had solid economic reasoning behind it—providing that most of the manufacturing equipment could itself be built on the Moon from lunar materials.

**Lunar Factories**

Not only was this possible, it was necessary.

Manufacturing at Moonbase made little economic sense if most of the basic equipment—jigs, fixtures, machine tools, etc.—had to be hauled from Earth. Moreover, because of the unique environmental conditions on the Moon, lunar factories are very different from their terrestrial counterparts. The

# 100-FOOT DIAMETER FACTORY

*Cross-section*

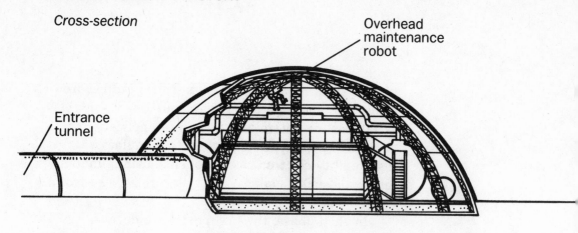

Overhead
maintenance
robot

Entrance
tunnel

*Overhead view*

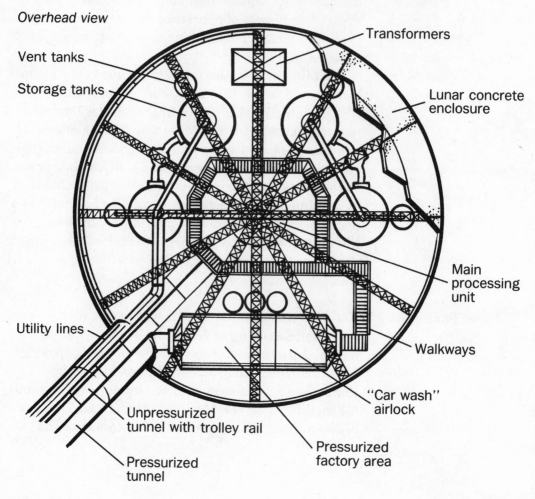

Transformers

Vent tanks

Storage tanks

Lunar concrete
enclosure

Main
processing
unit

Walkways

Utility lines

"Car wash"
airlock

Unpressurized
tunnel with trolley rail

Pressurized
factory area

Pressurized
tunnel

proper equipment for a lunar factory does not exist on Earth.

Lunar factories are mostly "out in the open," up on the surface. They are almost completely automated. The few machines that do not run under automatic, computer-directed control are teleoperated by human directors whose control stations are safely underground. The factory interiors are open to vacuum, except for small specialized areas where air is deemed necessary or desirable.

Newcomers to Moonbase often find it difficult to accept the idea that vacuum is a *beneficial* environment for most industrial operations. They instinctively regard vacuum as dangerous; and so it is—to humans. To properly designed machinery, including robots, vacuum can be extremely benign, largely because it is extremely clean.

Contamination is something that terrestrials (human beings who have always lived on Earth) take for granted. On a planet teeming with life from bacteria to whales, thick with pollution from human and natural sources, and deeply within a turbulent atmosphere that transports spores, dust, pollen, smog, moisture, and other pollutants all across the globe, cleanliness is a matter of degree.

In the $10^{-12}$ torr vacuum of the lunar surface, cleanliness comes virtually free. Not only is the environment free of external pollution sources, the contaminants *inside* materials can be removed quite easily. Metals, for example, usually have a certain amount of residual gases trapped inside them. In the one-trillionth of a torr environment of the Moon, these gases seep out of the metal's crystal structure and boil off into space. This process is called *degassing*.

Thus Moonbase's factories are open to vacuum. They are built on concrete platforms to keep them above the dusty surface of the regolith and covered by meteor shield domes of lunar honeycomb aluminum to protect them from the infall of microscopic meteorites. The largest source of contamination in these factories comes from the humans who must occasionally visit the facilities to do repair, maintenance, or alteration work that the robots are incapable of. All human factory workers must wear pressure suits, of course, in the airless areas. In addition, humans must enter the factory through special decontaminating airlocks, in which electrostatic "scrubbers" remove all particles of dust or dirt on the outside of their suits and special powdered detergents are applied to the suit exteriors to remove all traces of oil, perspiration, and other contaminants. Then the airlock is decompressed and the visitor waits in vacuum for a predetermined time before the hatch to the factory proper is unsealed. Some workers refer to the decontamination airlocks as "the car wash."

No human visitors are allowed to enter a factory area except through the decontamination airlocks. Each factory's security robots are programmed to prohibit visitors who try to enter a factory from the dusty regolith.

**Welding and Metalworking**

Another advantage of vacuum is that metals can be "cold welded." Ultraclean and degassed metals can be permanently joined merely by holding them to-

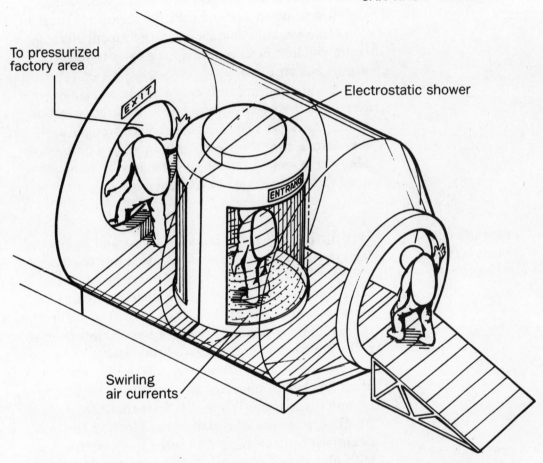

To pressurized
factory area

Electrostatic shower

EXIT

ENTRANCE

Swirling
air currents

gether, without the need for heat. Metals that self-weld easily are those with relatively low melting temperatures, including aluminum, tin, zinc, copper, nickel, iron, and silver. Self-welding can be a problem, however, when two pieces of metal that are not meant to be joined are accidentally brought together!

For other welding purposes, electron-beam welding equipment is used. On Earth, electron-beam welding is expensive and difficult because it must be done in a vacuum chamber. On the Moon, electron-beam welding is as commonplace as acetylene-torch welding is on Earth.

Metals that are difficult to shape or machine on Earth can be worked quite easily in lunar vacuum, mainly because such metals become stronger and less brittle once their contaminants have outgassed. Many ores can be refined by heat alone, without the need for exotic chemical treatments.

### Closed-Loop Manufacturing

One further difference between lunar and terrestrial factories is how wastes and pollution are handled.

On Earth, for thousands of years people have tended to dump their wastes in nearby streams and allow the smoke from their fires to drift away on the breeze. Only in the past century has environmental pollution become a vital terrestrial issue.

On the Moon, with no streams or air, waste-handling has been important since the very beginning of human occupation. While it is true that the original Apollo astronauts who visited the Moon in the mid-twentieth century tended to litter their landing sites with abandoned equipment, the people of Moonbase and Lunagrad are much more careful and caring about their environment.

Moreover, because all human habitats on the Moon *must* be self-contained, closed ecological systems, waste-handling is literally a matter of life and death.

There is also a practical, economic side to the problem of waste-handling and pollution. Since about 90 percent of human waste is water, it is essential to recover and recycle this most precious resource. In addition, because it was quite expensive to bring equipment and supplies from Earth, Moonbase's habitats and facilities were designed from the very beginning to recycle or otherwise utilize as much of their waste products as possible.

For example, as a byproduct of its oxygen-manufacturing process, the earliest Lunox facility produced a considerable tonnage of powdered iron and titanium oxide. This was not merely dumped on a waste heap; the metals were used as building materials for the construction of Moonbase and its outlying facilities. To this day, Moonbase's metal refineries are fed in large part by the "garbage" from the Lunox plants.

This is called "closed-loop manufacturing," and it is essential to Moonbase's economic viability.

**Raw Materials**  Raw materials for lunar manufacturing come from three main sources:

1. *Lunar ores* are strip-mined from the regolith. Both rocks and fines (powdered soil) are used. The major elements found in the regolith are oxygen, aluminum, silicon, titanium, iron, calcium, and magnesium. Useful amounts of boron, gallium, potassium, phosphorus, and rare earth elements have also been found. Metals heavier than iron are extremely rare, except in scattered sites of meteor strikes.

Lunar ores are the raw materials for production of glass, fiberglass, ceramics, semiconductors, concrete, metal sheets and beams, honeycomb metal sheets, and composite materials such as boron-fiber-reinforced ceramics.

2. *Earth imports* consist mainly of hydrogen and organic chemicals such as nitrogen and carbon, all of which are almost totally lacking on the Moon. A small amount of these three elements are available from pockets of ammonia ($NH_3$) and methane ($CH_4$) trapped beneath the floor of Alphonsus.

Hydrogen is necessary as feedstock for oxygen and water production. Carbon and nitrogen are vital for agriculture and life support, as well as inputs to certain manufacturing processes. The carbon reduction process, for example, is used to produce semiconductor materials for electronics systems and optical quality glass out of raw lunar silicon.

3. *Lunar-grown* resources include most of the food grown in Moonbase's farms and an increasing amount of organic waste material. Limited only by the available supply of water, lunar agriculture/ aquaculture not only feeds the population of Moonbase but provides feedstock for manufacture of plastics and pharmaceuticals. Moonbase provides most of the food for manned deep-space missions, and food exports to LEO stations are increasing each year.

A fourth source of raw materials, *imports from other bodies of the solar system,* is a small but growing part of Moonbase's economy. Water itself, as well as organics such as carbon and nitrogen, are available in comets. Metals, minerals, and organics exist in staggering quantities in the asteroids. At present efforts to use these resources are in their infancy. However, as more of Moonbase's resources are obtained from the comets and asteroids, imports from Earth will dwindle.

**Integrated Manufacturing**

No single manufacturing effort at Moonbase operates by itself. Every manufacturing cycle and facility is integrated into a carefully coordinated system that takes into account economic efficiency, raw material requirements, integration with other processes, output markets, manpower, productivity, recycling, and waste-handling.

Moonbase's manufacturing facilities are fully integrated to produce oxygen, water, various types of glass, metals, ceramics, construction materials, electronics components, and reinforced composites. Following the flow of inputs through the various manufacturing processes:

1. Undifferentiated lunar ores are screened, heated, and separated. Ilmenite is shunted to the Lunox facility, where it is put through the hydrogen reduction process to yield water and oxygen. The remaining iron and titanium oxide are sent to the metals refinery.

2. Ores other than ilmenite are moved by conveyor belt to a second separator. Fines are sent to the solar furnace facility where silicon is extracted for processing into glass products (insulation, building bricks, containers, tiles, etc.). Some of the glass, while still molten, is drawn off for use in the high-

quality optical glass manufacturing facility. Metallic elements in the fines are sent to the metal manufacturing facility.

3. Rocks are compacted into powder and separated into their constituent metals and silicon. The silicon is routed to the glass factory, while the metals are processed by several methods (including electrolysis and heating in a solar furnace) into castings, sheets, fixtures, etc. The iron and titanium oxide by-products of the Lunox facility and the metals rejected from the fines used in the glass factory serve as additional inputs here.

4. Rare elements such as boron and gallium are extracted from the ores and routed to the specialized facilities for manufacturing electronics components and composite materials.

5. Energy inputs for all processes are provided either by electricity or by heat. Electricity is generated in the solarvoltaic farms, with back-up power available from nuclear reactors. Approximately half the electrical power generated by the solarvoltaic farms is stored in superconducting coils during the day, for use during the long night when the solarvoltaic cells are inoperative.

Heat is obtained directly from sunlight during the lunar day. Solar furnaces, consisting of mirrors that focus unfiltered sunlight, can create temperatures of several thousand degrees at their focus. Solar furnaces are inoperative during the lunar night.

6. Waste heat created by any individual process is either radiated into the vacuum or recycled for use as energy input to other processes. Careful utili-

zation of waste heat during the 350-hour lunar night allows manufacturing processes to go on with only a small portion of the lost solar heat made up by standby electrical furnaces.

## Lunar Construction Materials

While oxygen was obviously the first product to be manufactured from lunar ores, construction materials were a very close second. As long as all structures for habitation and work had to be lifted from Earth, a permanent Moonbase was too expensive to consider. Therefore, among the earliest manufacturing experiments done on the Moon's surface were attempts to create useful construction materials from lunar resources.

*Concrete* is an excellent construction material. It is strong, fireproof, and can be made in almost any shape. In the one-sixth gravity of the Moon its strength-to-weight ratio makes it superior to most metals for construction purposes. Moonbase's Main Plaza vault, the platforms for the factories and spaceport, and much of the underground flooring and airtight bulkheads are made of lunar concrete.

Concrete is a mixture of cement and "aggregates": that is, small pieces of rock and sand. On Earth, water is an essential ingredient for cement. Rock and sand (fines) are plentiful on the Moon. Moonbase produces waterless cement entirely out of lunar resources. The ingredients are phosphates and anorthite from highland regolith. Lunar anorthite ($CaO.Al_2O_3.2SiO_2$) is low in calcium content for concrete formulations, but when heated to 3,000° C

(5,432° F) in the presence of phosphate ($Ca_3[PO_4]_2$) its calcium content can be enriched to approximately 50 percent by weight.

Phosphates are not abundant on the Moon, but the phosphate consumed in the reaction can be regenerated by heating the phosphorus byproduct of the cement reaction with pyroxene from maria regolith.

*Glass* is another useful and versatile material. Glass of every type—from building bricks to crystal to the finest optical quality—is produced at Moonbase from lunar silicon and solar heat.

While manufacturing glass bricks and tiles for construction purposes is a fairly straightforward operation, two special applications of glass have been developed at Moonbase that cannot be duplicated on Earth: large optics and Glassteel, a transparent glass with the structural strength of steel.

Glass is essentially a liquid that freezes at normal room temperatures. It is produced in the molten state, a mixture of silicon and other elements introduced to control the final quality, color, strength, etc., of the finished product. It is also shaped while molten, and then allowed to cool until solid and finished. On Earth it is extremely difficult to build large structures of glass—especially if they must be polished to an astronomically accurate smoothness, as for a telescope mirror—because Earth's gravity deforms the glass while it is still molten and may even crack the finished piece.

In the one-sixth gravity of the Moon it is possible to make much larger glass pieces of much higher purity and smoothness.

Moonbase has developed a simple process for manufacturing large optical-quality glass. Instead of making a telescope mirror, for example, and then grinding it for months to produce the necessary microscopic smoothness, a metal mold for the mirror is built and polished to the desired smoothness. The mold is allowed to degas in vacuum until it is ultrapure. Then molten glass is injected into the mold and allowed to cool and degas under controlled conditions.

Using this simple process, Moonbase has produced the main mirror for the 1,000-centimeter (393.72-inch) optical telescope at Star City, the telescope that has detected planets orbiting Barnard's Star and Wolf 359. Smaller optical components are an increasingly important export item. Moonbase Inc. is currently negotiating a contract to mass produce specialty lenses for Minolta Camera Co., Ltd., of Osaka.

The sweeping windows of Moonbase's main vault that offer such a breathtaking view of Alphonsus are made of Glassteel manufactured at Moonbase. Strong as the concrete of the vault, yet transparent as crystal, this glass/metal mixture could not be made on Earth.

## Semiconductors, Ceramics, and Plastics

A world that is 43 percent silicon dioxide should be a good place to manufacture electronics components, such as silicon-based semiconductors. Add a better vacuum than any obtainable on Earth, and it is obvious that the Moon has the perfect environment for manufacturing transistors and other electronics "chips."

Indeed, Moonbase manufacturers all its own electronics components and systems, and silicon-based semiconductors were one of Moonbase's earliest export products. Today, improved electronics components based on gallium chips are replacing the silicon products.

In the clean vacuum of the Moon, microscopic electronics chips are manufactured in automated facilities. The technique of depositing the electronically active material on a chip in a thin film has been refined to the point where the film may be only as thick as a single molecule.

Silicon in the regolith is still used to manufacture solarvoltaic cells that convert sunlight directly into electricity. Solar energy farms spread over considerable portions of Alphonsus's floor and the "shore" of Mare Nubium, outside the ringwall mountains. Mobile, automated solar cell factories mounted on specially modified crawlers continuously add new sections to the energy farms, converting the regolith ore into finished solarvoltaic cells and connecting them to Moonbase's electrical power grid.

Silicon and heat from solar furnaces are also used to manufacture a growing range of ceramic materials. Ceramics are used within Moonbase for piping, heat exchangers, storage tanks, and structural elements such as bricks. Because refractory ceramics can withstand high temperatures, they make excellent insulating materials, including spacecraft heat shields and even rocket nozzles, when combined with special metal alloys.

Such metal-ceramic mixtures, called *cermets*, are difficult or impossible to produce on Earth. They can best be manufactured in the near-zero-gravity environment of an orbiting space station. Moonbase's materials scientists and engineers have developed techniques for manufacturing cermets in one-sixth gravity at costs considerably lower than those incurred at LEO. Plans are underway to test a pilot-plant facility in the L1 station that would combine the advantages of microgravity with lower raw material costs.

For almost the first full decade of its existence, Moonbase's two largest imports from Earth were food and plastic sheeting. The plastic was necessary mainly to provide airtight seals in areas where people lived and worked. Plastic sheets were heat-bonded together and attached to rock or structural walls to form airtight barriers against the vacuum.

The development of lunar agriculture helped ease the need for such imports. Not only did the farms provide a constantly increasing percentage of the food at Moonbase, but they provided the raw material for manufacturing plastics. Special sections of the farming areas were set aside for crops such as soybeans that could provide both high-protein nutrition for people and animals, and feedstock for the fledgling plastics manufacturing facility as well.

Plastics have many uses. Temporary shelters are made of plastic tents reinforced with wire mesh to withstand the load of radiation-shielding rubble placed atop them. Mirrors of enormous size are made of plastic sheet spray-coated with lunar aluminum, to make them reflective. The only communications satellites allowed to orbit the Moon are passive balloons made of aluminized plastic that reflects microwave radio beams; these satellites are completely radio-quiet on the far side, where radio noise would interfere with the search for signals from extraterrestrial intelligence.

Lunar plastics, ultrapure because they are manufactured in vacuum, are also used for the *solar sail* spacecraft that drift outward through the solar system, pushed by the pressure of sunlight, carrying scientific instruments for studying the planets and their moons, the asteroids, and the interplanetary medium.

**Sandwiches and Diamonds**

Two other lunar products are important to Moonbase's economy: metal honeycomb sandwiches and gemstones.

Metal honeycomb "sandwiches" were first developed nearly a century ago, on Earth. Two sheets of metal are separated by a honeycomb of thin metal walls that trap pockets of air inside them. Honeycomb sandwiches can be very thin and light, yet have the structural strength of much thicker sheets of metal. They were widely used in aircraft and spacecraft construction as early as the 1960s.

In space, honeycomb sandwiches can be produced in which the pockets between the sheets are no longer filled with air, but with vacuum. This makes the honeycomb an excellent insulator against heat or cold, as well as a strong lightweight material.

Moreover, in low gravity honeycomb materials

can be made of metal "foams," in which molten metal is bubbled with gas, then rolled into sheets and allowed to degas in vacuum. Not only can this be done with metals: honeycomb sandwiches have been produced at LEO and Moonbase from pure ceramics, cermets, ceramic-plastic combinations (called *cerplasts*), glass, and metal-glass combinations.

Moonbase's gemstones come from two sources: natural and manmade.

The Moon has been bombarded by meteorites since the very beginnings of the solar system. Some of these meteorites contain natural diamonds—pure crystallized carbon—within them. The first lunar diamond was discovered by a research technician who was sawing open a meteorite fragment that had been found on the surface of Mare Nubium. When her diamond saw snapped, the technician was stunned to find that a small glittering object embedded in the meteorite had broken it. The object was a perfect blue-white diamond, one-tenth of a carat in weight.

The Moon is literally covered with such gemstones, albeit sparsely. A popular pastime for tourists and Moonbasers alike is to go "diamond hunting" on the surface. There are real diamonds mixed into the regolith, and they are much easier to find than on Earth (although still it is not truly easy).

Gemstones are also grown at Moonbase. Crystals grow larger and more easily in low gravity than on Earth. At Moonbase, small chips of diamond are used as "seeds" to grow industrial quality and even gem-quality stones. Methane is passed over the seed chips at a temperature of 2,000° C (3,632° F). The gas decomposes into hydrogen (which is used else-where) and *monatomic* carbon—individual carbon at-oms—which deposit themselves on the seed chip and literally grow into large diamonds. The process is greatly facilitated by the clean conditions of lunar vacuum, the low gravity, and the absence of vibra-tion. (The gemstone facility is built on special shock-absorbing mounts to guard against even the slightest moonquakes.)

Diamonds, rubies, sapphires, and other precious stones are manufactured not only for jewelry; they are much more widely used in industrial machinery and in devices such as lasers. Other kinds of crystals for electronics chips and high-quality optical lenses are also manufactured at Moonbase.

**The Competitive Edge**

Moonbase has swiftly evolved from a "mining town" into a highly advanced center for manufacturing.

As has happened throughout Earth's history, the factories that depend on lunar resources can operate more economically if they are as close as possible to those resources. While factories at Moonbase cannot make use of zero gravity, for most industrial pur-poses one-sixth *g* is almost as good. In addition, Moon-base has zero-gravity conditions available at the L1 space station, where specialized manufacturing proc-esses are located.

The tide of economic competition is strongly in favor of Moonbase. Manufacturing operations at LEO are migrating to Moonbase. At the current rate of change, within another decade LEO will be used only for those processes that absolutely require zero-gravity conditions.

**Career Growth Opportunities**

Employees of the Mining and Manufacturing Program Office tend to move into the administrative divisions of the Department of Management more than any other program office's employees. This is because Mining and Manufacturing is deeply involved in the economic lifeblood of Moonbase, trade with LEO and Earth. M&M staff members are constantly striving to improve existing Moonbase export trade products and invent new ones.

M&M's personnel include geologists, geochemists, mining engineers, factory managers, machinists, teleoperators, computer analysts, metallurgists, plastics chemists, chemical engineers, cryogenics engineers and technicians, crystallographers, electronics engineers and technicians, production engineers and technicians, optics engineers and technicians. Academic credentials range from PhDs in the geological sciences to special degrees from technical institutes.

Mining and Manufacturing interfaces closely with virtually every other aspect of Moonbase's operations, from Space Transportation to Exploration and Research. The opportunities for cross-training are extensive.

Many M&M employees take courses in management and business as they see the opportunities for moving into the administrative services.

# Exploration
and Research

Men first came to the Moon in search of knowledge. Since those very earliest days, since before there was a Moonbase, the quest for knowledge has been a driving force in the human exploration and settlement of the Moon.

Today, Moonbase's Exploration and Research Program Office directs a scientific studies across a broad range of astronomical, selenological, physical, social, and medical sciences. Scientists make use of the Moon's low gravity, high vacuum, seismic stability, wide temperature range, and—on the far side—low radio noise, to conduct experiments and make observations that are impossible anywhere except on the Moon.

Ongoing studies include:

> Origin of the solar system
> Astronomy
> Sun/Earth/Moon interactions
> Particle physics
> Ultrapure chemistry
> Engineering sciences
> Medical sciences
> Life sciences
> Agricultural sciences
> Lunar exploration

Moonbase cooperates fully with Lunagrad in virtually all of these investigations. There is a vigorous ongoing exchange program in which scientists from Lunagrad work at Moonbase for weeks or months at a time, while Moonbase scientists do the same at Lunagrad. Moonbase and Lunagrad share the costs of operating Star City, at the Mare Moscoviense. The far side facility is staffed equally by men and women from both lunar communities.

**Origin of the Solar System**

Until the Age of Space began, questions about the origin of the solar system could be approached only by passive observations of the Sun, planets, and minor bodies, and geological investigations of Earth and meteorites that were found on Earth. Today, scientists are examining the structure of the Moon, Mars, and certain comets and asteroids firsthand, as well as studying the Sun and other planets and moons from space and lunar observatories.

To this day, scientists are uncertain as to how the Moon formed and how the solar system began. Before the first lunar landings it was hoped that the Moon's surface rocks, never eroded by wind or rain, would reveal information dating back to the very beginnings of the solar system. However, it was quickly determined that the Moon does suffer a weathering effect from the constant infall of meteoric dust. And, as a glance at the battered face of the Moon easily shows, the surface was subjected to a tremendous meteoritic bombardment in the early history of the solar system.

Lunar geologists (selenologists) have determined that the Moon was formed between 4.5 and 5 billion years ago. The heavy meteoritic bombardment ended some 3 billion years ago, although meteorites of smaller sizes, ranging down to dust grains, constantly hit the lunar surface. The oldest rocks found on the Moon are about 4.7 billion years old; the youngest, about 3.1 billion.

Geological teams are methodically studying every square centimeter of the lunar surface. Their goal is to produce a surface map that reveals not only the geographic features, but the types of geological formations and their chemical content. This information is important for understanding the origins and history of the Moon. It is also invaluable in locating and identifying new sites of valuable natural resources. Much of this work is done by automated surface crawlers. Teams of human geologists are sent only to specially interesting sites that their robotic aides have found.

Seismologists are investigating the inner structure of the Moon. Working in cooperation with colleagues from Lunagrad, Moonbase's seismologists have established a network of seismological stations that stretch from the walled plain Plato (51°N, 9°W) to the giant crater Clavius (56°S, 14°W) and eastward to the Mare Crisium (60°E). These stations, which operate under remote control from Moonbase and Lunagrad, include both passive seismic detectors that measure natural moonquakes, and active explosive charges that allow the scientists to study how a measured amount of energy affects the lunar crust and interior.

Seismic stations have also been established on the far side, from the Cordillera Mountains on the rim of Mare Orientale (20°S, 110°W) to Star City itself in Mare Moscoviense (27°N, 147°E). Because of objections from Star City's astronomers to manmade vibrations that might effect their equipment, only passive seismic observations are made on the far side.

Measurements of heat flow from the lunar interior are also made at the seismic stations. They have shown conclusively that the Moon does have a small molten core, presumably of iron.

Lunar geologists are also studying the mascons that underlie several of the larger maria. These massive concentrations of dense material are believed to be the remains of huge meteorites that blasted out the maria early in the Moon's history, more than 3 billion years ago. The mascons lie, on the average, between 50 and 80 kilometers (30 to 50 miles) below the surface. They measure some 5 kilometers (3.1 miles) thick and between 100 and 200 kilometers (62 to 124 miles) in diameter.

The fact that the mascons have not sunk to the center of the Moon indicates that the lunar rocks were solid, not molten, when they hit and blasted out the maria. The mascons undoubtedly contain megatonnages of heavy metals, but because they are buried so deeply, it is easier (at present) for Moonbase to mine heavy metals from asteroids than to engage in very deep pit mining.

The regolith contains some rocks and fines that are slightly magnetic, although the Moon as a whole has a negligible magnetic field. Radioactive elements in KREEP*-type and other rocks are found only in certain locations, such as around the Mare Imbrium basin. Does this mean that these elements are not "native" to the Moon, but were carried here by meteoroids? Since the Moon is deficient in elements heavier than iron, this seems a likely explanation.

Geologists also help in the study of the Sun's

---

*KREEP: Potassium (chemical symbol K), Rare Earth Elements, and Phosphorus.

history. For billions of years the solar wind and cosmic radiation have bathed the lunar surface with subatomic particles. Geological teams drill deeply into the Moon's crust and take core samples that contain minute amounts of these particles, trapped in the lunar regolith and crust. The number of particles trapped at different levels, and the relative abundances of the various kinds of particles, give important data on the Sun's behavior in the past.

Thus by investigating the structure of the Moon, scientists are learning more about the early history of the Moon and the Sun, and probing the origins of the entire solar system, as well.

**Astronomy from the Moon**

For centuries astronomers complained that studying the universe from ground-based observatories on Earth was like trying to study the lights of a distant city from the bottom of the ocean.

The first astronomical observation to be made beyond the Earth's turbulent layers of cloudy air were conducted in unmanned high-altitude balloons in the 1950s. By the late 1980s the Hubble Space Telescope began to revolutionize astronomy. This 94-inch optical telescope, orbiting nearly 400 kilometers (about 250 miles) above the Earth's surface, operated 24 hours a day and was never blocked by clouds, haze, city lights, or atmospheric turbulence.

Astronomy moved to LEO during the final decade of the twentieth century and the first decade of the twenty-first. There are still many fine astronomical facilities in Earth orbit, both manned and unmanned, but the Moon has become the astronomer's

mecca. The finest equipment and the best astronomers do their most exacting work at Moonbase, Lunagrad, and especially at Star City (Zvezdagrad) on the
lunar far side.

The Moon offers many advantages over Earth-
based and orbiting astronomical facilities.

The lunar surface provides a solid and stable
platform for precise astronomical observations. The
slight seismic disturbances of moonquakes are actually less of a problem than the vibrations produced
by truck traffic at many Earthbound observatories.
Orbiting observatories are extremely sensitive to vibrations and other motions because they are effectively in zero gravity. Lunar observatories have the
advantage of one-sixth gravity: low enough to allow
construction of very large mirrors and antennas;
high enough to avoid the problems of vibration, motion, and pointing accuracy that affect facilities in
zero gravity.

The Moon's 27-day rotation rate allows astronomers to keep their instruments fixed on pinpoint tar-
gets for hundreds of hours at a time, which cannot
be done at orbiting facilities or on Earth's surface.

Most orbiting astronomical facilities are within
the Earth's magnetosphere. Those in LEO are below the Van Allen radiation belts. This limits the
studies that can be made of the solar wind and interplanetary magnetic field dynamics. The Moon is far
beyond the Earth's magnetosphere, except for one
period each month when its orbit carries the Moon
through the Earth's geomagnetic "tail." At that
time, detailed studies of the magnetosphere tail are
conducted.

The far side of the Moon is the quietest place in the solar system, as far as radio-frequency noise is concerned, with 3,476 kilometers (2,155 miles) of lunar rock insulating against the radio clamor from Earth. During the periods of night on the far side, even the natural radio emissions of the Sun are thoroughly blocked out. When the planet Jupiter is not in the far side's night sky, the radio emissions of the distant stars can be studied with practically no interference whatsoever.

## THE FIRST E.T. SIGNALS

The discovery of the first radio signals from deep space that may be the work of intelligent extraterrestrials was made not by a human being, but by the IBM/NEC Mark XVIII supercomputer. The machine, located at Star City's astronomical facility, analyzed millions of data inputs from the radio telescopes and separated the faint, periodic signals from the background "noise" of natural astronomical radio emissions.

The signals appear to emanate from a region of the Sagittarius Arm of the Milky Way galaxy that is veiled from direct view by an extensive interstellar dust cloud.

Further analyses by the Mark XVIII and other supercomputers on Earth have concluded that the signals are unlike any known natural radio emissions, and that they resemble human language in their periodicity and repetitiveness. To date, however, all attempts to translate the signals into an intelligible message have been fruitless.

The area from which the signals originate is about 10,000 light years away, which means that the signals being received now were transmitted some 10,000 years ago.

As Moonbase astronomer Herman Scott pointed out, "Conversations will tend to drag when there's 10,000 years between saying, 'How are you?' and getting back, 'Fine. And you?' "

Star City, therefore, has become the prime center for SETI: the search for extraterrestrial intelligence. Several very faint radio signals that are periodic in nature have been detected by Star City's complex of radio telescopes. These signals are being studied to determine if they actually are deliberate messages from an intelligent civilization. They appear to be emanating from the Sagittarius arm of our Milky Way galaxy, a region that lies some 10,000 light years* closer to the center of the galaxy than our solar system.

There are three major radio telescopes at Star City: the Drake telescope, a 90-meter (295-foot) steer-

---

*A light year is the distance that light travels in a year. Light travels in space at a speed of nearly 300,000 kilometers (186,000 miles) per second. Since there are approximately 31.5 million seconds in a year, a light year is 9.46 trillion kilometers (5.87 trillion miles). The star nearest our solar system, Alpha Centauri, is 4.3 light years away. The center of the Milky Way galaxy is some 30,000 light years from us. The great spiral galaxy in Andromeda, the farthest object the unaided human eye can see, is more than two million light years away. The Moon is about 1.3 light *seconds* from Earth.

able "dish" antenna, the largest in the solar system, and two 50-meter (164-foot) dishes, named Shklovsky and Sagan. The facilities are named in honor of Frank Drake, I. S. Shklovsky, and Carl Sagan, three twentieth-century pioneers in the search for extraterrestrial intelligence.

The 50-meter Sagan antenna is located not at Star City itself, but in the large crater Apollo (37°S, 153°W), some 2,600 kilometers (1,612 miles) away. It operates under remote control from Star City and is normally attended by automated robotic systems. Working together, two antennas can conduct radio interferometry studies that require a long baseline. The longer the baseline between two telescopes, the smaller the angular distance they can resolve. Star City's radio telescopes were able to pick out from the natural background of radio noise of the stars the periodic microwave emissions from the region of Sagittarius that may be intelligent signals.

For *very* long baseline radio interferometry, Star City's facilities work with radio astronomers on Earth, providing a baseline of approximately 384,405 kilometers (238,331 miles). Only experiments in which one of the radio telescopes is aboard a spacecraft beyond the orbit of the Moon have provided longer baselines.

The largest optical telescope in the solar system is Star City's 1,000-centimeter (393.7-inch) Bok reflector, named after the Dutch-American astronomer, Bart J. Bok. Like the radio telescopes, it was built entirely on the Moon, from lunar materials. The main mirror for the Bok telescope was built at Moonbase, as were most of the optics. The structural frame was built by a joint Lunagrad-Moonbase team on-site at Mare Moscoviense.

The Bok telescope was able to resolve the planets orbiting Barnard's Star and Wolf 359, the first time that planets of other stars were actually observed, rather than deduced from indirect data.

Other astronomical facilities at Star City include a growing array of instruments designed to detect forms of radiation or subatomic particles that cannot be observed from the surface of Earth. Thanks to the airless vacuum of the Moon, all forms of radiation in space reach the lunar surface. And since the Moon has a negligible magnetic field, solar and cosmic particles can be detected on the surface, as well.

Telescopes sensitive to infrared, ultraviolet, X ray, and gamma ray wavelengths gather data at Star City.

Other instruments seek to detect the elusive neutrino, a subatomic particle that can penetrate a thickness of more than a hundred *light years* of iron without being stopped! Neutrino "telescopes" consist of large vats of chlorine-rich water buried several meters underground. Billions of neutrinos from the Sun and deep-space sources stream through the vats each second. On very rare occasions, a neutrino will strike a chlorine atom in just the right way to transmute it into an atom of radioactive argon. This activates sensors in the tank, which record the event. Neutrino astronomers are correlating the rate of neutrino flux recorded on the Moon with the results from decades of observations on Earth, where neutrino telescopes are located in deep mines, kilometers below ground.

Astronomers are also recording gravity waves produced by the collapse of massive stars, deep in space. The first verified detection of gravity waves was made at Moonbase in 2008, even before the formal dedication of the base. It was the first major scientific discovery made on the Moon, and it verified the predictions of Einstein's 1916 general theory of relativity. It is believed that the gravity waves detected on the Moon originate in galaxies far beyond our own Milky Way. Gravity-wave observations can be made much more easily on the Moon, where background vibrations from moonquakes are much less of a problem than earthquakes, volcanic eruptions, and manmade disturbances.

In addition to providing an extremely rich treasure of new observational data for astronomers and cosmologists, Moonbase's astronomical teams also furnish important data for more immediate and practical purposes. Observations of comets and asteroids,* for example, are used to determine where needed natural resources can be most easily obtained.

An "asteroid patrol" system has been established, in which radar facilities automatically scan the sky to detect asteroids on trajectories that could

---

*The terms *asteroid* and *meteoroid* are often confused and confusing. An asteroid is a small body in orbit around the Sun, a minor planet. Asteroids range in size from several hundred kilometers to dust motes. The word means "little star," and some astronomers insist that the correct name for them is *planetoid*. A meteoroid is an asteroid that is on a collision course with a larger body, such as the Earth or the Moon. A *meteorite* is the remains of a meteoroid found on the ground after impact. A *meteor* is the flash in the sky seen when a meteoroid hits the Earth's atmosphere and burns up: it is a "falling star." Since the Moon has no atmosphere, there are no meteors on the Moon. But plenty of asteroids become meteoroids, hit the Moon, and then are known as meteorites.

impact on the Moon or Earth. If an asteroid large enough to cause significant vibrations in the lunar crust is discovered, Star City is alerted to suspend observations requiring ground stability for the period during which its impact would create unacceptable vibrations. The only "down time" resulting from such an impact, to date, was one hour and eleven minutes, when a three-meter-wide metallic asteroid struck Mare Serenitatis at high velocity. With only a small molten core to absorb such impact energy, the Moon's solid crust "rang like a gong," in the words of a lunar geologist.

Such events are vanishingly rare. It was after that event that the asteroid radar patrol was established. No other asteroid large enough to cause damage to a lunar facility or to Earth has yet been detected. If one is, however, Moonbase has the expertise and equipment to make a deep-space rendezvous with the intruder and alter its trajectory to the point where it will not strike the Earth or the Moon.

---

THE RISK OF BEING HIT
BY A METEOROID

Astronomers have calculated that the chances of being hit by a meteoroid large enough to penetrate the skin of a lunar hard suit are approximately one in ten trillion. Actual observations of meteoritic infall rates show that meteoroids large enough to penetrate the shielding over a Moonbase factory strike the Moon once in roughly every 50,000 years. Since the factories and other facilities on the Moon cover only a minute portion of the 40,000,000 square kilometers (15,000,000 square miles) of the lunar surface, the chances of damage from a meteoroid strike are negligible.

**Sun/Earth/Moon Interactions**

The Moon is an ideal "laboratory" for studying the delicate interactions of the Earth–Moon system with the solar wind.

As early as 1896 the Norwegian physicist Olaf K. Birkeland suggested that the Sun might be emitting streams of particles such as electrons and protons that cause the auroras—the Northern and Southern Lights—when they interact with the geomagnetic field and strike the uppermost layers of the Earth's atmosphere. By the early 1960s spacecraft had proved conclusively that there is a solar wind of ionized particles streaming outward from the Sun. It is a *plasma* that consists mainly of electrons and protons.

## THE FOURTH STATE OF MATTER

On Earth we are familiar with solids, liquids, and gases. In space a fourth state of matter exists, which physicists call *plasma*. A plasma is a gas that is ionized: that is, some or all of its atoms have been stripped of their electrons. Thus a plasma consists of the negatively charged electrons and the positively charged atomic nuclei (called ions) that have lost electrons. In most plasmas, some un-ionized atoms are also present. While a plasma is electrically neutral *as a whole*, because the electrons and ions balance each other, the plasma can still conduct electrical currents and be influenced by magnetic fields. A plasma can also be called an ionized gas. But while ordinary gases are not affected by electromagnetic forces, plasmas are.

The solar wind normally passes the Earth–Moon area at a velocity of some 400 kilometers per second (about 250 mps), although when a violent flare erupts on the Sun the wind can reach "hurricane strength" velocities five times that speed. By terrestrial standards the solar wind is an excellent vacuum, less than $10^{-12}$ torr; it contains no more than 10 to 100 particles per cubic centimeter (about the volume of a sugar cube) as compared to the $10^{19}$ particles per cubic centimeter of normal room-temperature air.

The Earth, encompassed by its magnetosphere, creates a shock wave in the solar wind, somewhat like the bow wave of a boat as it cuts through water. But the shock wave in the solar wind is not made by the solid body of Earth; it is made by the magnetic field of the magnetosphere. The solar wind presses against the magnetosphere, flattening it to some extent on the sunward side and stretching the night side out into an enormous "tail" that goes past the orbit of the Moon.

The solar wind strikes the Moon's surface, since there is no lunar atmosphere or large-scale magnetic field to absorb or deflect it. However, for about one-quarter of its orbit around the Earth, the Moon is within the geomagnetic tail, and is shielded from the flowing solar-wind plasma.

Thus studies of the solar wind and its effects on the geomagnetosphere can be conducted from the Moon's surface. As the ionized particles strike the lunar surface they create an electric field some 5 to 10 meters (16 to 33 feet) high. While this electric "sheath" is too weak to be of interest to anyone but plasma physicists, it does present one practical problem—it tends to make dust particles from the lunar soil cling electrostatically to space suits and equipment. In some cases it becomes necessary to "ground" equipment to remove clinging dust grains.

Plasma scientists have "piggybacked" detectors and particle sampling sensors to the seismic stations deployed across the lunar surface. Plasma sensors have also been installed in the towers that support the lunar cable car systems, where they have the advantage of being above the electric sheath, for the most part.

**Particle Physics**  The two most powerful particle accelerators in history allow physicists to probe the fundamental nature of matter and energy on the Moon. One of the accelerators is manmade, the other is natural.

The natural accelerator is located deep in space, perhaps beyond the Milky Way galaxy altogether. The particles it accelerates, which have been somewhat misnamed as cosmic rays, are the most energetic bits of matter that physicists have yet studied.

Physicists measure the energy of subatomic particles in terms of electron volts. One electron volt is the energy acquired by an electron when it moves through an electrical potential of one volt in a vacuum. It is a tiny bit of energy. But cosmic rays have been measured at energies of billions ($10^9$), even hundreds of billions ($10^{11}$), of electron volts and higher.

On Earth, cosmic ray particles from deep space tend to strike atoms in the atmosphere, creating a shower of secondary particles and even tertiary particles that eventually reach (and even penetrate) the ground. On the Moon, *primary* cosmic particles reach the surface and can be measured and studied directly.

These particles from deep space consist mainly of the nuclei of atoms that have been stripped of their orbital electrons, plus a few free electrons. Cosmic particles have relatively more heavy elements than the universe as a whole does, which leads to the conclusion that they are remnants of aged stars that have exploded. Such stars are called *supernovas*. However, the mechanism for accelerating the particles to such enormous energies (their velocities approach the speed of light) is far beyond the energy of a typical supernova. Somewhere in deep space there is fantastically powerful particle accelerator. Or perhaps more than one.

## RELATIVE ABUNDANCE OF ELEMENTS

| Element | In universe | In cosmic rays |
|---|---|---|
| Hydrogen | 10,000 | 10,000 |
| Helium | 1,500 | 700 |
| Lithium, boron, beryllium | $10^{-5}$ | 15 |
| Carbon, nitrogen, oxygen, fluorine | 1.5 | 40 |
| Neon—potassium | 0.2 | 14 |
| Heavier elements | 0.1 | 5 |

While manmade particle accelerators have not equaled the enormous energy output of the stars, Moonbase can boast a particle accelerator that briefly speeds subatomic bits of matter to energies higher than all but the most powerful of cosmic rays.

A particle accelerator is basically a vacuum through which subatomic particles are accelerated by powerful magnets to velocities close to the speed of light, plus sensors and measuring equipment that record what happens when the accelerated particles are smashed into a target—usually other accelerated particles moving in the opposite direction.

The Moon offers the best vacuum available to scientists, and Moonbase already has powerful magnets in operation as part of the mass driver that catapults unmanned payloads off the lunar surface. In fact, the mass driver was originally developed out of research aimed at building better particle accelerators; the wheel of serendipity has turned full circle on the Moon.

Since particle physics experiments actually take place in a few seconds or less, it is not difficult to divert the energy of the mass driver to powering a particle accelerator experiment. Of course, preparing for an experiment run may take hours, days, weeks, or more. Special facilities have been built to generate the particles desired for study and to store them until the moment of the experiment. Storage rings of superconducting magnets hold the particles in "racetrack" orbits until they are injected into the accelerator.

The Moonbase accelerator has achieved energies of one hundred trillion electron volts ($10^{14}$eV, or 100,000 BeV).

Among the other physics experiments being conducted at Moonbase is an attempt to determine the lifetime of the proton. Theoretical considerations have indicated that the proton may not be a stable particle, although its lifetime is longer than the age of the universe. If the proton is unstable, it means that the universe will eventually dissolve.

On Earth, because of background "noise" from natural sources of radioactivity and secondary cosmic rays, the limit of sensitivity of these experiments is $10^{33}$ years. At Moonbase's underground laboratories the background noise is reduced to the point where proton decay lifetimes of $10^{35}$ years have been measured. To date, the proton seems quite sturdy and the universe should last for a long, *long* time.

One other experiment that could have enormous consequences for the human race is the ongoing effort to measure hypercharge, the fifth fundamental force that theoreticians believe may work counter to gravity.

Very precise experiments performed in the low gravity and airlessness of the Moon have indicated that hypercharge exists, although it is by far the weakest of the five fundamental forces of nature— weaker even than gravity itself. Work is now underway to determine the exact strength of hypercharge, and to consider ways in which it might be turned to practical use.

If hypercharge can be harnessed, then an effective "antigravity" machine may be possible. Space flight, as well as many other aspects of human life, would be revolutionized.

## Ultrapure Chemistry

The advantages of an ultraclean environment for chemical research have allowed Moonbase to develop new metal alloys, composite materials, foam ceramics, metal-reinforced glass, and new electronics materials.

Most of these products and processes are protected by patents or held proprietary by Moonbase Inc. They are not to be discussed with the general public or potential competitors. However, the general principles of lunar chemistry are clear to see.

Lunar vacuum allows metals and other materials to degas, clearing them of contaminants down to a very low level. In the cryogenic cold that is so easily available on the Moon, chemical processes can be slowed to the point where the reactions between individual molecules can be studied. New processes and refinements of known processes can be developed.

One area of crucial importance has been Moonbase's development of superior electronics materials and components. For decades, electronic "chips" have been produced by depositing a thin film of semiconductor material on a substrate. The substrate acts as a structural frame on which the electronically active semiconductor is supported. Moonbase has developed thinner, lighter, yet stronger substrate materials and new processes for thin-film deposition that have resulted in the new technology of molecular electronics, or *molectronics*, as it has come to be called.

A molectronic pilot manufacturing plant is now being built, under the supervision of the Exploration and Research Program Office, with consultation by the Mining and Manufacturing Program Office. If pilot production of molectronic components meets expectations, the Mining and Manufacturing Program Office will assume operational responsibility for the plant and enlarge it to a full-sized production facility.

**Engineering Science**

A small but active group within the Research Program Office still devotes its efforts to exploring new ways in which lunar materials can be used for practical purposes.

It was the Engineering Sciences group that developed the techniques for making lunar concrete, foam ceramics, and the plasma torch system for lunar excavation. This group also supervised construction of the Moonbase particle accelerator and its associated equipment.

At present the Engineering Sciences group's major effort is construction of Moonbase's second mass-driver facility, in cooperation with the Space Transportation Program Office. Continuing research is underway in cryogenics, electrical power generation and storage, and construction techniques.

## Medical, Life, and Agricultural Sciences

Although Medical, Life, and Agricultural Sciences are separate groups, each with their own agenda of research goals, their work is so interdependent that it is useful to consider them together rather than separately.

All three groups are devoted primarily to supporting the human habitation of Moonbase and its outlying facilities. The closed-loop environmental systems that provide the base's air, water, heat, and food are almost entirely self-sufficient. While imports of hydrogen (or water) and biologically necessary volatiles such as carbon and nitrogen are still needed for Moonbase's existence, these elements are increasingly imported from asteroids and comets, making Moonbase less dependent on terrestrial sources. Not only does this increase Moonbase's viability as a self-sufficient center for human habitation, it also has a beneficial effect on the economy of Moonbase.

Ecologically, Moonbase is in the unique position of *requiring* growth. This may seem paradoxical at first, but the larger Moonbase becomes, the easier it is to maintain a closed-loop ecology. The planet Earth is an example of a closed-loop ecology: air, water, food, etc., are constantly recycled on a very large scale. Moonbase is still too small to be able to "close the loop" entirely. But as Moonbase continues to grow, its recycling systems will become less dependent on technological equipment and more capable of using "natural" systems such as green plants for recycling the air and bacteria for recycling water and other wastes.

One field in which the medical and life science programs of Moonbase are preeminent is geriatrics. For more than two decades, Moonbase has maintained a small but steadily growing retirement community for men and women who are too infirm to survive in Earth's heavy gravity and polluted atmosphere. In the low gravity and clean air of Moonbase, most of these people do not merely survive, they become active members of the community. Several have begun entirely new careers.

**Lunar Exploration**     Although human beings have been living continuously on the Moon since the beginning of the twenty-first century, explorers are still combing the lunar surface and still making new discoveries.

Most of the explorers are robots, automated or remotely controlled crawlers making their way across the rugged landscape. Unmanned satellites crisscross the Moon, also, their sensors mapping the surface and probing for natural resources.

Human exploration teams have reached both lunar poles and circumnavigated the Moon on its surface. Although none has yet discovered water in any form, the explorers have found valuable sites of resources ranging from precious stones such as diamonds to deposits of gallium, sulfur, methane, and ammonia—which, on the Moon, are more valuable than gemstones.

**Moonbase University**

With such a high percentage of scientists and other professionals among Moonbase's population, it was inevitable that a university would arise.

Moonbase University was founded in 2023. It is mainly a research center, rather than a teaching institution. The staff consists of permanent Moonbase residents, with visiting faculty from among the temporary employees. Guest lecturers include leading figures in every academic field, some specifically invited to Moonbase, others giving special lectures from Earth via interactive television. No undergraduate instruction is offered at the University, but graduate degrees can be obtained in fields such as low-gravity physiology, astronomy, selenography, and other areas associated with Moonbase's expertise.

Moonbase University is accredited by more than fifty nations, including each of the fifteen nations that are major share holders in Moonbase Inc. The University enjoys close ties with Lunagrad Technical Institute and maintains electronic links with most of the major universities on Earth.

**Career Growth
Opportunities**

As one wag put it, the Exploration and Research Program Office engages in both "pure research and impure research." That is, while much of the work done by E&R involves fundamental scientific studies aimed at increasing humankind's knowledge of the universe, there is also a good deal of applied research aimed at specific goals such as finding new sites of natural resources and developing new industrial processes.

The Exploration and Research Program Office boasts more doctorate degrees than any other department of Moonbase. More than eighty percent of E&R's people hold advanced degrees in science or engineering, mainly in the fields of astronomy, astrophysics, geophysics, plasma physics, selenology, seismology, particle physics, theoretical physics, astrochemistry, radio astronomy, SETI, planetary astronomy, chemistry (with emphasis on vacuum chemistry), low-gravity physiology, osteopathy, geriatrics, cardiovascular research, biology, plant and livestock genetics, and ecology.

You may be one of the increasing number of new PhDs who have chosen to do your postdoctoral research at Moonbase, drawn here by our unmatched scientific staff and "out of this world" facilities.

Thanks to the close interactions among specialists in different disciplines, you will find ample opportunity to broaden your interests and abilities, no matter what your level of education and training. For example, several Moonbase chemists have made important contributions to techniques of semiconductor manufacturing, and have gone on to play major roles in the Mining and Manufacturing Program Office. Moonbase geologists and astronomers have worked closely with both the M&M and Space Transportation Program Offices in the ongoing effort to identify new sites of natural resources on the Moon, asteroids, and comets.

Moonbase encourages such interactions, and offers our fine educational facilities to help "cross-fertilize" ideas and expertise among the various scientific disciplines.

# Footprints in Moondust:
# Lunar Tourism

A century ago, the very thought of reaching the Moon was widely regarded as impossible. "Flying to the Moon" was considered the ultimate nonsense of wooly-headed dreamers. Even when the first astronauts landed on the lunar surface, 1969–72, there was widespread criticism: the Apollo program was called a worthless stunt, a "Moondoggle."

As recently as a decade ago, the idea of tourists vacationing on the Moon was considered absolute nonsense. Who would want to travel a quarter-million miles to visit a world of barren desolation? Scoffers claimed that the costs, the dangers, and the lack of comforts would forever keep the Moon off-limits to tourism.

How wrong they were!

But the doubters were not proven wrong merely by good fortune. Moonbase management drew careful plans, more than decade ago, to assess the possibilities of lunar tourism. Several interlocking factors convinced the planners that lunar tourism could be feasible.

First, living space at Moonbase was being rapidly expanded. Quarters for tourists could be provided that were as comfortable as accommodations at first-rate tourist hotels anywhere on Earth.

Second, services for tourists opened up an entirely new area of employment for Moonbase. In particular, many of these services could employ teenage or young adult men and women. Not only would this allow Moonbase to begin recruiting younger personnel, helping to balance the age demographics of the base, but it could be used to encourage older personnel with teenage children to come to Moonbase with their families. Many key scientists, technicians, and administrators were attracted to Moonbase for this reason.

Third, transportation costs were being driven down steadily by Moonbase's oxygen production and manufacture of spacecraft structures, components, and electronics systems.

**Tourism Program Office**

Once the decision was made to "go after" tourists, the Tourism Program Office was established. Its first task was to convince the most influential segments of the terrestrial tourist market that Moonbase was attractive and affordable.

This was done by resorting to one of the fundamental ploys of the tourism industry: well-known personalities, considered "trend setters" in their societies, were invited to Moonbase gratis. They included famous figures from the worlds of entertainment, sports, and the media. Within two years Moonbase was established as a "dream vacation site."

**Flying Like a Bird**

There are two things that a person can do on the Moon that are impossible on Earth. One of them is human-powered flight. In one-sixth gravity, all that is needed to fly is a set of wings and some air. The Tourist Program Office provides the wings, and flying space is available inside the vault that covers the Main Plaza.

Although it appears superficially like hang gliding, lunar flying is true human-powered flight. It does not depend on wind or air currents, but on the muscles of the flier. Using nothing but one's own muscle power, a person can lift off the ground, climb, bank, soar, even do spectacular aerobatics in the gentle lunar gravity.

The wings used for flying are made of monolayer plastic, manufactured in zero-gravity facilities at LEO, and braced with ultralightweight struts made of lunar magnesium. They can be rented at the Tourism office in the Main Plaza.

## The First Footprints Club

The other thing that a vacationer can do on the Moon that cannot be done anywhere on Earth is literally to plant his or her booted feet "where no man has gone before."

Because the topmost layer of the regolith is powdery, with about the consistency of beach sand, you leave footprints wherever you walk—footprints that will last for millions of years if they are not disturbed by others.

The First Footprints Club is a loosely organized association of those people who have made footprints on the lunar surface. Moonbase has set aside tracts of ground for First Footprints along the floor of Alphonsus and outside the crater's ringwall, on the Mare Nubium.

A visitor (or a Moonbase employee) can leave his or her footprints in one of these tracts and place a small nameplate of lunar metal alongside them. They are then sprayed with instant-setting clear plastic

so that they cannot be disturbed. The person registers
the exact lunar latitude and longitude of the prints
with the First Footprints Club, which maintains
such records at its headquarters at Moonbase.

Footprints at historical sites, such as the Apollo
11 landing area at Mare Tranquillitatis, are covered
with protective plastic so that visitors cannot damage them.

**Shrines and
Scenic Wonders**

By far the most popular place on the Moon for visitors is the Apollo 11 landing site, Tranquility Base.
The base of the Lunar Module remains exactly
where Armstrong and Aldrin left it when they lifted
off to rendezvous with Michael Collins, orbiting the
Moon in the Apollo Command Module. The American flag still stands stiffly in the airless silence. The
equipment and sensors that the astronauts used remain exactly where the first men on the Moon left
them.

There are other shrines on the Moon, as well.

The Borkovsky landing site of 1999, inside the
giant crater Copernicus, offers not only history but a
chance to see one of the largest, most prominent, and
most beautiful craters on the Moon.

Two of the original temporary shelters from the
Heroic Years have been preserved in their original
condition for tourists and other visitors. One of them
is on one of the walking paths laid out on the floor of
the crater Alphonsus. The other is on Mare Nubium,
and is reachable by tour bus or trolley.

The landing site of the Diana 1 mission of 2001

is not only within half a kilometer of the Apollo 12 lander (1969); the earlier unmanned Surveyor 3 spacecraft is also sitting a scant 200 meters (about 650 feet) from the Apollo landing module.

From this spot on Oceanus Procellarum, towards the end of a long lunar night, you can almost believe that this broad expanse of rock *is* an ocean. The ground undulates gently, like the swells of a calm sea frozen forever into stone. In the soft glow of Earthlight, this lunar ocean appears grayish-green in color, almost like the deep seas of Earth.

Then the Sun comes up and bathes the area in merciless harsh light. You begin to realize that you are on a vast desert of stone. Lunar rilles snake across the regolith here and there and, of course, there are the inevitable craters of every imaginable size. Rocks are strewn about as if some giant's child had left his playthings behind.

Scenic wonders abound on the Moon. A few hours' ride from Alphonsus is the Straight Wall, a 130-kilometer-long (80-mile-long) cliff jutting up from the plain of Mare Nubium. The rocky wall rises some 250 meters (800 feet) from the mare, at an angle of more than 40 degrees. Far to the north is the Alpine Valley, a rift some 120 kilometers long (75 miles) in the Lunar Alps, along the northeastern edge of Mare Imbrium. Ranging in width from roughly 6 to 10 kilometers (about 4 to 6 miles), the valley seems almost to have been dug out deliberately to connect Imbrium with Mare Frigoris.

On the way to the valley, many visitors stop to view Mt. Pico, towering in splendid isolation 2,400 meters (7,900 feet) above the plain of Mare Imbrium. Pico is one of the few lunar mountains that stands virtually alone, rather than as part of a mountain chain.

Another favorite site of visitors is the crater Opelt, where the DelCorso expedition was finally rescued. Since Opelt often serves as the halfway point for the annual Moonbase crawler race, there are several abandoned crawlers to be seen in the area. Naturally, the craters that are most prominent from Earth, such as Copernicus, Kepler, and Tycho, attract many visitors. Most of these natural wonders are reached by ballistic rockets ("lobbers"), since overland traverses would take many days.

Many of the historic shrines of the Moon can be reached by cable car or special crawler "buses" operated by the Tourist Program Office. The buses can accommodate up to a dozen tourists and are usually staffed by a crew of three. They are equipped for overnight trips and are completely self-sufficient, with life support systems, hard suits, provisions, and communications gear.

Special bus tours offer a week-long jaunt along the route of the original Mason, Lenoire, and Wayne traverse across the rim of Mare Imbrium. Stop-offs to view Mt. Pico, the Alpine Valley, and the lovely crater Copernicus are available. Lunar "camp" sites along the route have been improved and enlarged, and now serve as overnight stops for tour groups as large as twenty persons.

**Moonwalks**

One thing a lunar vacation offers that is hard to find on crowded Earth is *solitude*. There are a total of some five thousand people on the Moon, at the most. The Moon's surface area is about the same as that of North, Central, and South America combined. There is plenty of room to "get away from it all."

While Moonbase employees are generally forbidden from walking on the surface alone, there are specially reserved areas where tourists (or employees) are allowed to walk on the surface by themselves. These Moonwalk Lanes are all inside the floor of Alphonsus, and extend for some 200 kilometers (125 miles) along the inner rim of the ringwall and across the floor to the central peak.

For Moonwalking, or any outdoor activity, hard suits are available at a nominal rental fee. These pressure suits offer complete protection against the vacuum and temperature extremes of the lunar surface, and are armored against radiation. They are completely equipped with a twelve-hour supply of air, drinking water, two-way radio, and emergency survival/rescue kit.

While on Earth a hard suit would weigh more than 250 kilograms (550 pounds), it weighs less than 50 kilograms (110 pounds) in the Moon's one-sixth gravity. Even so, the suits are powered by servomotors that amplify muscle movements, so that they are quite easy to move in. (See the "Quality of Life" chapter, p. 99, for more information on hardsuits.)

The lanes meander across Alphonsus's pitted floor, following the flattest and safest ground, skirting the rilles and craterlets that make much of the floor too treacherous for visitors to walk. One of the popular destinations for Moonwalks is the wreckage of the Ranger 9 spacecraft, which "hard landed" near the ringwall 24 March 1965 as part of the preliminary photoreconnaissance of the Moon undertaken in preparation for the Apollo program.

The Moonwalk lanes are clearly marked, and lined with emergency stations every kilometer. The stations include oxygen, telephone links, and a protective safety capsule (bizarrely nicknamed a "coffin") which can hold two persons in hard suits for 24 hours, in case a suit is ruptured or its life support equipment breaks down.

(There have been unconfirmed reports that safety capsules have occasionally been used as "love nests." Such unauthorized use of safety equipment could endanger the life of a tourist or employee, and is grounds for employee dismissal.)

**Lunar Recreations**  With the exception of activities that require large bodies of water, such as sailing or waterskiing, virtually every sport played on Earth can be played on the Moon—with a difference.

It could be said that astronaut Alan Shepard was the pioneer of lunar sports when, in 1971, he hit a golf ball with a club improvised from the handle of a piece of geological equipment and a six-iron head he had brought with him, along with the ball. Reports vary as to how far his drive went, and the Moonbase employee who eventually found Shepard's ball discreetly refrained from measuring the distance of the shot.

Today visitors to Moonbase (as well as employees) can engage in a wide range of sporting activities—although "outdoor" sports are discouraged, for safety reasons, with the exception of Moonwalks and mountain climbing.

**Mountain Climbing**

Years before the Tourism Program Office was started, the Moonbase Safety Division frowned on efforts to climb the ringwall mountains that circle Alphonsus. Yet the wall had to be surmounted regularly, since Moonbase itself is built into the inner face of the western arc of the mountains, while much of the mining and industrial work has to be done on the Mare Nubium, on the other side of the ringwall.

A cable car system was established for hauling freight and personnel over the ringwall, while plans for boring a tunnel through the mountains were developed, studied, and eventually put aside.

In the meantime, sizable teams of Moonbase personnel climbed the mountains as part of their jobs. Some of them liked it well enough to start mountain climbing for enjoyment. Word of this spread quickly throughout the base, and soon there were unofficial competitions among Moonbasers to see who could scale the highest peaks in the shortest times.

Faced with such realities, the Safety Division made a virtue of necessity and began to organize the mountain-climbing efforts, providing guides, mapping routes of various difficulties, and offering instruction on climbing techniques.

Once the Tourism Program Office opened its doors, close liaison was established with the Safety Division's mountaineers, so that vacationers could have the opportunity of scaling Alphonsus's ringwall mountains.

From the crater floor, the ringwall rises in a series of terraces to crests that average about 3,200 meters high (10,500 feet). The tallest peak, Mt. Yeager, is 3,752 meters (12,310 feet).

Mountain climbing on the Moon is rather different from its terrestrial counterpart. The advantage of lighter gravity is offset by the necessity of wearing a hard suit. Lunar mountains generally are less rugged than terrestrial ones. While the tallest mountain chains on Earth are less than a few hundred million years old, most lunar mountains were formed three billion years ago or earlier, and have been eroded by the constant infall of micrometeorites and the huge swing of temperature extremes between the lunar day and night. Thus, while most lunar slopes are not as steep as those found among the terrestrial Alps, Rockies, Andes, or Himalayas, they tend to be smoother and more difficult to scale than comparable grades on Earth. Some climbers have characterized certain slopes as "slick," or even "glassy."

Alphonsus was formed slightly more than three billion years ago, according to the best geological evidence. While its ringwall mountains are challenging to the newcomer, there are much higher peaks elsewhere on the Moon. Special climbing tours are arranged by the Tourist Program Office to the Lunar Apennines, where Mt. Bradley rises 4,400 meters (14,400 feet).

The tallest lunar peaks are in the Leibnitz Mountains, near the south pole, where crests exceeding those of the Himalayas abound. Only special teams of professional climbers are allowed there, since the slopes are too difficult for amateurs and tourist facilities are not available in that rugged sector.

The tallest mountain in the solar system is Olympus Mons, on the planet Mars. At 27,000 meters (88,583 feet) it is three times higher than Earth's Mt. Everest. No one has scaled Olympus Mons—yet.

**Other Sports and Recreations**

Many of the athletic activities we are familiar with on Earth have their lunar counterparts. Any sport that involves heavy physical activity, however, looks to the newcomer as if it is being played in slow motion, because of the lower gravity of the Moon.

Swimming in the recreational pool of the Main Plaza is little different than swimming on Earth, although diving is *very* different. Incredible dives from the 30-meter (99-foot) platform are made even more spectacular by the dreamlike slow motion induced by low gravity.

On Earth, falling objects accelerate at the rate of 32 feet per second each second (32 ft/sec²). On the

Moon, they fall at the rate of 5.28 ft/sec², some six times slower than on Earth.

Jai alai is an excellent example of the difference between our two worlds. Often called "the fastest game on Earth," lunar jai alai is at the same time faster that its terrestrial counterpart—and slower. The ball bounds off the walls even faster than on Earth, since it weighs less yet is still propelled by Earth-evolved muscles. But the players can leap to fantastic heights and come back down slowly, dreamily in the gentle lunar gravity. As a result, Moonbase's jai alai courts are much larger than those on Earth, and some Moonbase residents can "out play" professional terrestrial athletes.

Volleyball, tennis, handball, basketball, and many other games are similarly altered by the Moon's gentle gravity. This allows virtually anyone who wants to a chance to participate. Since a person can jump much higher on the Moon than on Earth, volleyball nets and basketball hoops are usually placed at least three times higher than they would be Earthside.

**Moonbase Cuisine**  Vacationers are often surprised by the variety and quality of food available at Moonbase.

Two first-class restaurants offer varied menus ranging across European, Oriental, and American traditional dishes. Virtually all the victuals, with the exception of a few specialty items, are grown at Moonbase's farms. Wines and alcoholic beverages, however, are imported and consequently somewhat more expensive than in most major terrestrial cities.

**Career Growth Opportunities**

If you have come to Moonbase to work in the Tourism Program Office, the chances are that you are a high school or undergraduate college student who is traveling with your parent(s). Unless, of course, you are already a professional in hotel management, recreational services, food and beverage services, a paramedical or paralegal specialist, or a psychologist.

Professional members of the Tourism Program Office interact frequently with Moonbase Hospital and medical research staff, particularly in ongoing studies of human physiological and psychological reactions to low gravity and artificial environments.

Students who serve as tour guides, junior hotel personnel, or in other areas of the Tourism Program Office have an unparalleled opportunity to see the Moon and to further their education while doing so. You can participate in the full range of Moonbase's educational offerings, and work with the teachers, scientists, engineers, and administrators who staff Moonbase. You can see for yourself what living and working at Moonbase is like, and perhaps you will decide to return to Moonbase when your Earthside education is finished.

# Luniks: Permanent Residence

The first person to decide to stay on the Moon permanently was an Argentinian astronomer, Dr. Eduardo Mullen.

"My work is here, my life is here," he said quite simply. Although most of his working time is spent at Star City, he is a Moonbase resident and teaches regularly at Moonbase University.

The permanent residents of Moonbase and Lunagrad refer to themselves as "Luniks." They have formed the first community of humans to live permanently off the Earth.

**Applying for Permanent Residency**

Since Moonbase is not a sovereign nation, each permanent resident retains citizenship in his or her native country. However, permanent residents vote on issues before the Governing Council and increasingly it is these permanent Luniks who are filling the Council's posts.

If the idea of permanent Moonbase residency interests you, there are several important steps you can take:

1. Do your job well. Excellent job performance is the most important criterion used to assess applicants for permanent residency.

2. Cross-train in the job areas and disciplines that interact most strongly with your own. With a population of only 2,000, Moonbase cannot afford narrow specialists among its permanent residents. We need men and women whose interests and abilities span more than one field. Moonbase manage-

ment and your fellow employees will be more than happy to help you learn new skills, and Moonbase's educational services are available to further your quest for knowledge.

3. Actively participate in Moonbase's social and political life. Permanent Luniks are "doers!"

4. Pick a permanent resident to advise and guide you, and to sponsor your application for permanent residency when the time comes.

To be accepted as a permanent resident, a person must have worked at Moonbase or Lunagrad for at least five years. Moonbase's Governing Council must accept the person's application, and the Moonbase Administration must agree that resources and living space are available for the applicant and any member of his or her immediate family included in the request for permanent residency.

If the person's nation of origin (or citizenship) objects to the person remaining permanently on the Moon, the dispute is adjudicated in the World Court, where the person is represented by the Legal Division of the International Astronautical Authority. Only three such cases have arisen (including Dr. Mullen's precedent-setting case) and all have been settled in favor of the individual who wants to remain at Moonbase.

To date, there are 191 permanent Moonbase residents, slightly under 10 percent of the base's total population. This percentage is remarkably stable: although an average of ten persons per year apply for permanent residency, Moonbase's growth is such that the number of temporary employees also tends to expand at about 5 percent per year.

## THE FIRST BURIAL ON THE MOON

The first person to be buried on the Moon was Orlando Chavez, former president of the United States and one of the earliest permanent residents of Moonbase.

Chavez was the first president to visit the Moon during his term of office, and officiated at the formal opening of Moonbase on 20 July 2020. A former astronaut, he applied for permanent residency after his second term in the White House ended in January 2025. By unanimous vote, the Governing Council waived the usual requirement that a person serve at least five years working on the Moon before being considered for permanent residency.

President Chavez became an active contributor to the tourism program before succumbing to cancer in 2029. He willed his body to be buried in one of the Moonbase farms, stating, "I want my mortal remains to be of use, recycling my carbon and volatiles into the soil. I'll still be a part of this community that I have grown to love, even after death."

Many permanent residents have followed President Chavez's eloquent example in their wills.

**Physical and Psychological Effects**

If you someday decide to live at Moonbase permanently, you'll find that in many ways, the Moon is a better place to live than Earth.

The low lunar gravity, the clean environment

FIRST LUNAR BABY

The first baby on the Moon was born 16 May 2011 to Russian physician Ilena Markova, the wife of Igor Gregorovich Markov, a Soviet political officer at Lunagrad. Valentina Markova weighed 2.52 kilograms (5 pounds, 9 ounces) at birth.

Lunagrad's medical facilities were limited to a four-bed infirmary at the time, intended to deal only with accidents or unexpected illnesses. Dr. Markova was actually in charge of the infirmary. She professed that she had not realized she was pregnant when she left Earth, and once on the Moon she did not want to risk a return flight until the baby was safely delivered.

She supervised her own delivery and was back on the job running the infirmary the day after Valentina's birth. Dr. Markova, her husband, and their infant daughter left Lunagrad in December 2011 and have lived in Baikonur, not far from the major Soviet spaceport of Tyuratam, ever since.

free of most pollutants and allergens, the community of intelligent, highly motivated men and women of all nationalities, races and religions, make Moonbase an ideal place to live.

People who are infirm on Earth, due to age or disease, can lead active, useful lives in the one-sixth gravity. Even for normally healthy men and women, lunar gravity can be exhilarating. Some physical problems arise when a person accustomed to low gravity must return to Earth, but for permanent residents this is no longer a matter of concern.

Children have been born at Moonbase. With one exception, they have been born to temporary employees. Long-term medical studies of pregnancies, childbirth, and infant growth show that there are no deleterious effects due to the low lunar gravity. Sociological and psychological studies have concluded that children being reared at Moonbase show much the same behavior patterns as children growing up in a university environment on Earth.

While pregnant women were not allowed to participate in the early exploration of the Moon, the development of spaceplanes that take off and land horizontally, like an airplane, means that spacecraft are no more dangerous to fly in than terrestrial commercial airliners. Pregnancy is no longer a hindrance to coming to Moonbase, although pregnant women are not allowed to work on the lunar surface.

**Large-Scale Immigration**

Although Moonbase does permit men and women to live on the Moon permanently, we do not allow true immigration. No one has emigrated from Earth merely because he or she wanted to live on the Moon. All of Moonbase's permanent residents originally came here as employees on temporary contracts. It is only after a minimum of five years of working at Moonbase or Lunagrad that a person can be considered for permanent residence.

Moonbase is not a retirement community. Permanent residents are expected to perform some community service, no matter what their age.

Many teach, either at the university or at the public schools that serve the temporary employees' children. Others remain in their original jobs, or have become entrepreneurs in a wide variety of endeavors. Permanent residents have turned to painting, creating jewelry from lunar gems, prospecting for new resources, operating restaurants (mainly for the tourists), and various forms of entertainment, including dance, drama, and music.

Most of the prospectors seek that "El Dorado of the Moon," water. None have succeeded, as yet. But they still search. Although international law forbids private ownership of lunar resources, Moonbase policy is to award the finder of any new site of raw materials one-quarter of the profits generated by the resources.

All prospecting missions must be approved by the Safety Division, which is responsible for checking the physical health of the individuals involved and the conditions of their equipment and supplies. Prospectors must file their mission plans with the Geology Section of the Exploration Division.

Yet, inevitably, the question of large-scale immigration must be faced. As space transportation costs continue to decline, as Moonbase continues to expand and prosper, retirement to the gentle gravity of the Moon will become more and more attractive to many on Earth.

Already, Moonbase has received proposals from several developers, offering to construct small retirement communities on the Moon on an experimental basis. The communities would be similar to the facilities now available for tourists, although the men and women who live in them would be permanent residents. The Governing Council has expressed strong reservations about allowing such development at Moonbase, and corporate management has rejected the proposals on the grounds that life support facilities would be severely strained by an influx of retirees (with their servants and medical attendants) who do not participate in Moonbase's economic lifestream.

However, as water from asteroids and/or comets becomes more readily available, the establishment of self-sufficient retirement communities may begin to look more attractive. One proposal is to revive the original concepts of Gerard K. O'Neill and other early space enthusiasts and construct very large habitats at the libration points along the Moon's orbit, L4 and L5. Such habitats, large enough to house hundreds of thousands, could provide a completely Earthlike environment inside them, even to the extent of open grassy fields, woods, lakes, and streams. Their gravity fields could be controlled by their rate of spin: lunar or even lower gravity could be achieved easily.

Constructing habitats at L5 or elsewhere will be the largest engineering task of the space age. Capital investment will necessarily be very high, but the technical and financial risks of such an endeavor are far lower now—thanks to Moonbase's capabilities and experience—than they were when the concept was first broached by O'Neill more than half a century ago.

# Facing the Future

In 1912, when the state of Arizona was admitted to the U.S., its first senator, extolling the virtues of his state in a very long speech, ended by saying, "In short, gentlemen, all that Arizona needs to make it Heaven is water and society."

Another senator was heard to whisper, "That's all that Hell needs to make it Heaven!"

Water and society. The limit to Moonbase's growth as a community is the availability of water. Water is the key to Moonbase's self-sufficiency.

The search of water on the Moon itself continues. Moonbase's ongoing geological exploration program will eventually investigate every square centimeter of the lunar surface and probe deeply into the crust. Private entrepreneurs, in teams or individually, also search for water and other resources.

Thanks to Moonbase's unique combination of natural advantages, highly skilled and motivated work force, and growing industrial capacity, the search for water is now expanding throughout the inner solar system. Despite relatively high costs, it is estimated that water and other volatiles obtained from asteroids and/or comets will allow Moonbase to become fully self-sufficient within the next five years. At that point, the only materials imported from Earth will be luxury items—and people.

In direct contrast to the immigration policies of an earlier century on Earth, Moonbase does not seek "your tired, your weak, your poor." The men and women who come to Moonbase are the best and brightest of our home world. They come from every nation, and they are allowed to work at Moonbase only after psychological screening tests have assured that they are not hampered by racial or religious prejudices. It is from this stock that our permanent residents are drawn.

Far from being a lonely, hazardous, uncomfortable outpost at the fringes of civilization, Moonbase is swiftly growing into a center of excellence and achievement, a safe and comfortable home where men and women can live and work in harmony and peace.

What will the next ten years bring?

The exploration of the Moon will be completed over the next decade. The entire lunar surface will be mapped, detailed chemical analyses will determine the composition of the entire regolith, and seismological probes will produce a relatively complete understanding of the composition and dynamics of the Moon's interior.

Water and other volatiles such as nitrogen and carbon will be imported from near-approach asteroids and/or comets, ending Moonbase's dependence on imports from Earth.

Moonbase's manufacturing capabilities will increasingly be devoted to building deep-space vehicles, both manned and automated, capable of journeying out to the Main Asteroid Belt. Preliminary explorations of the Belt show metal, mineral, and volatile resources many times larger than the entire Earth can provide.

Astronomical studies of the universe will continue, with special emphasis on the faint radio signals emanating from the Sagittarius region of the Milky Way. If these signals are found to be the product of intelligence, attempts will be made to establish communications.

Three star probes will be launched toward Alpha Centauri, Barnard's Star, and Wolf 359. Although ten years from now the probes will still be nearly four decades away from their destinations, their sensors should be able to send a wealth of information about the planets orbiting the latter two stars.

The exploration of the remainder of the solar system will continue. Moonbase, in conjunction with Lunagrad and terrestrial universities and governments, will continue to support the human teams on Mars and in orbit around Mercury, and the robots probing Venus, Jupiter, and the outer planets.

The recent success on Earth of bringing thermonuclear fusion power plants on-line to produce electricity at competitive commercial rates will soon bring great changes to Moonbase's electrical power production. Terrestrial fusion power plants run on deuterium, an isotope of hydrogen found in water. Advanced fusion reactors can use tritium and helium-3, isotopes that do not exist on Earth but are abundant in the clouds of Jupiter. Automated spacecraft will scoop these isotopes from the Jovian atmosphere and return them to Moonbase, where advanced fusion power plants will provide abundant electricity through the lunar nights.

Moonbase itself will continue to grow. Inevitably,

as our population expands and our dependence on terrestrial imports lessens, the people of Moonbase will decide to apply to the United Nations for membership as an independent state. Preliminary discussions with key leaders among the fifteen-nation consortium that now owns the majority of Moonbase Inc.'s stock have indicated that they would raise no major objections to Moonbase's political independence, as long as Moonbase operations remain profitable.

In ten years we will see an independent Moonbase, rich in water and society: peopled by healthy, motivated men and women who will raise their families here and make Moonbase their home; known throughout the solar system as a center of excellence and a happy, thriving community; sparkling with beautiful pools of fresh water and glistening fountains that splash lazily in the Moon's low gravity; alive with human joy and achievement.

That is our goal. You can help to make it happen.

# Appendices

## 1. A Different World: Basic Lunar Facts

History of the Moon

Astronomers still cannot agree on how the Moon was formed. Some believe it was once a part of the Earth that broke away, very early in the history of the solar system, before the planets had formed solid crusts. Others theorize that the Moon originally formed far distant from Earth, somehow moved close to our home world, and was captured by Earth's gravity, and became a satellite of Earth. A third opinion holds that Earth and Moon originated pretty much where they are today: close but separate.

No matter how the Moon was created, it is hard to imagine a world more different from Earth, despite the fact that the Moon is closer to Earth than any other natural astronomical body.*

The Moon was created along with the Earth and the other major bodies of the solar system some 5 billion years ago. The oldest rocks of Earth, as well as meteorites that scientists have studied, and the so-called "Genesis Rock" discovered by the Apollo 15 astronauts, all appear to be from 4 to 4.5 billion years old.

Everything about the Moon is the result of its comparatively small size. Only one-quarter the diameter of Earth, and nearly half as dense, the Moon's surface gravity is one-sixth that of Earth. This means that the Moon is unable to hold an atmosphere, and thus is completely airless. While this poses problems for life support, it offers great advantages as well: Moonbase has become *the* prime center for

---

*With the exception of Toro, a tiny moonlet that circles the Earth at the L4 position along the Moon's orbit.

---

## PHYSICAL FACTS

| | Moon | Earth |
|---|---|---|
| Diameter: | 3476 kilometers (2,160 miles) | 12,742 kilometers (7,918 miles) |
| Mass: | 0.0123 | 1.000 |
| Density: | 3.34 grams/cm$^3$ | 5.11 grams/cm$^3$ |
| Surface Gravity: | 0.17 | 1.000 |
| Orbital Velocity: | 1.6 km/sec (0.99 mi/sec) | 7.9 km/sec (4.9 mi/sec) |
| Escape Velocity: | 2.38 km/sec (1.48 mi/sec) | 11.18 km/sec (6.94 mi/sec) |
| Length of Day: | 27 days, 7 hours, 27 minutes | 23 hours, 56 minutes |
| Mean Distance from Earth: | 384,405 kilometers (238,331 miles) | —— |
| Atmosphere: | None | Oxygen, nitrogen, carbon dioxide, water vapor, etc. |
| Highest Surface Temperature: | 134° C (273° F) | 58° C (136° F) |

---

| | Moon | Earth |
|---|---|---|
| Lowest Surface Temperature: | −153° C (−243° F) | −89.4° C (−129° F) |
| Magnetic Field: | negligible | 0.5 gauss |

*Note:* Orbital velocity is the speed needed to attain an orbit around the body in question; escape velocity is the speed required to leave that body completely.

natural resources and space transportation primarily because it is much cheaper to launch payloads from the Moon's surface than from the surface of Earth, with its heavy gravity and thick blanket of atmosphere.

Surface Features

The Moon's surface is composed of four major kinds of features:

*Mountains*, which are much like mountains on Earth. Although they have not been weathered by wind or rain, they have been eroded by the constant infall of meteoric dust, eons of alternate baking in the daylight and freezing each night, and the continual minor seismic activity that rattles the Moon's crust.

Most of the mountain chains have been named after mountain systems on Earth: the Apennines, the Carpathians, the Alps, etc. The Leibnitz chain, near the south pole, has several peaks higher than Mt. Everest.

*Regolith*, the surface layer of the Moon, consists of rocky debris originally ejected from volcanic explosions and the impact of large meteorites. Over the eons since these violent events, much of the rock has been pulverized into a fine powder by the constant infall of smaller meteorites (ranging in size down to dust particles) and the effects of intense heating during the fourteen-day-long lunar day and equally intense cooling during the fourteen-day lunar night.

Soft as beach sand on the surface, the regolith quickly hardens to rocklike consistency a few feet below. The regolith averages a few meters deep in the lunar plains, but can be considerably deeper in the mountainous uplands. Beneath the regolith lies the rocky crust of the Moon. The regolith's surface is strewn with rocks and boulders, and pockmarked by craters of all sizes.

*Craters* can range in size from tiny pinpricks to gigantic structures such as Bailly, in the southwest corner of the Moon's near side (the side always facing Earth), which is 295 kilometers (183 miles) across. A crater that size on Earth would stretch from New York City to Baltimore, or from Los Angeles halfway to San Francisco.

Lunar craters are usually named after famous scientists or philosophers, such as Copernicus, Archimedes, Kepler, and Plato. Since the establishment of Moonbase, small craters that cannot be distinguished from Earth have been named after prominent members of the lunar community, such as DelCorso, Brudnoy, Davis, and Rawlings.

Most craters on the Moon were created by the impact of meteorites, although some are probably the result of lunar volcanism. In the earliest era of the solar system, when the planets were forming out of smaller bodies, all the planets and their moons must have been bombarded heavily by very large meteoroids. The planet Mercury and the Moon, neither of which has any appreciable atmosphere, both show the scars of this bombardment. So does Mars, to a lesser extent. On Earth the constant weathering of wind and rain has erased most of the evidence of the bombardment, although a few ring structures called *astroblemes* still exist in North America, Africa, and elsewhere.

Some of the largest lunar craters, such as Plato and Aristarchus, are called *walled plains*, in part because they lack the central mountain peak of the large true craters.

Several large craters are the centers of bright "rays" of material streaking outward across the lunar surface. Most notable among these are Tycho, Copernicus, and Kepler. The rays are composed of rocks and pulverized material ejected from the crater, presumably when it was formed by meteoritic impact. Thus the rayed craters are undoubtedly younger than most other surface features.

*Maria*, or seas, were thought from ancient times to be bodies of water. They are the dark areas of the Moon's face that can easily be seen by the unaided eye from Earth. Telescopic observations, however, eventually showed that the "seas" are waterless. Even so, the maria have received fanciful names such as the Sea of Rains, the Ocean of Storms, and the Sea of Clouds.

The maria are large flat plains of basaltic rock that were originally molten lava. Whether the lava came from lunar volcanoes or was created by the titanic impact of very massive meteorites is still a subject of argument among selenologists. Most likely both causes were at work, eons ago when the maria were formed. The main period of lava flow apparently ended about three billion years ago.

Many of the maria have concentrations of massive material beneath them, which are called *mascons*, and were first discovered when the earliest artificial satellites placed in orbit around the Moon showed slight disturbances in their orbital paths. Mare Imbrium (Sea of Rains), Mare Crisium (Sea of Crises), Mare Orientale (Eastern Sea), and several others are the sites of mascons. Although selenologists have shown that the mascons are rich sites of heavy metals, the ores lie too deep for commercially feasible mining—at present. Studies are now underway to determine if these resources can be developed in the foreseeable future.

The largest of the lunar maria is Oceanus Procellarum (Ocean of Storms), which extends nearly 1,500 kilometers (930 miles) north to south. Mare Imbrium is 1,300 kilometers (806 miles) across, and Mare Orientale, much of which is on the lunar far side and cannot be seen from Earth, has a diameter of 965 kilometers (598 miles).

The Moon's Interior

Unlike the Earth, which has a considerable core of molten metal (mostly iron), the Moon is almost completely solid throughout. Seismic evidence indicates that the Moon has a small metallic core about 1,000 to 1,200 kilometers below the surface (about 620 to 745 miles) that may be hot enough to be molten.

The surface layer, or regolith, contains shattered

and pulverized rock fragments. Beneath this is a rocky lunar crust that averages some 60 kilometers (37 miles) thick. There is a sharp boundary at this level; below the boundary is the lunar mantle, which consists mostly of basaltic rocks. The maria are considered to be composed of dark basalts that poured out onto the surface when the crust was punctured, either by volcanic eruptions or the impact of large meteorites. The mantle extends down about 150 kilometers (93 miles), below which is the metallic core.

The composition of the lunar rocks is as follows:

*Regolith.* In the highlands, mainly plagioclase-type rocks, which consist of light-colored, glassy, brittle crystals that contain feldspar minerals such as albite (a mixture of sodium, aluminum, silicon, and oxygen) and anorthite (calcium, aluminum, silicon, and oxygen). These rock types are generally called *anorthosites.*

In the maria, the rock fragments include more of the dark basalts, such as pyroxene and olivine, which contain elements such as oxygen, silicon, titanium, iron, magnesium, aluminum, sodium, and calcium. Compared to terrestrial basalts, lunar basalts are generally low in sodium and potassium, but contain more titanium.

Maria basalts also include highly radioactive rocks called KREEP, which are rich in potassium (chemical symbol K), rare earth elements, and phosphorus.

*Crust.* Generally rich in anorthosites, similar to the highland regolith materials.

*Mantle.* Dense rocks of basaltic pyroxene and olivine, similar in chemical composition to the basalts of the maria. The maria are thought to be composed of mantle material that became molten and flowed along the surface.

*Core.* Metallic, although with a lower concentration of elements heavier than iron than the core of Earth.

## TYPES OF LUNAR ROCK

| Name | Chemical Composition | Found In |
|------|----------------------|----------|
| Plagioclase | Calcium Aluminum Silicon Oxygen | Highlands regolith and crust |
| Anorthite | (a type of plagioclase) | " |
| Pyroxene | Calcium Magnesium Iron Silicon Oxygen | Maria regolith and mantle |
| Olivine | Magnesium Iron Silicon Oxygen | " |
| Ilmenite | Iron Titanium Oxygen | " |

## Composition of the Moon

While different types of lunar rocks and strata have differing chemical compositions, the *overall* chemical composition of the Moon is as follows:

$$SiO_2 = 43\%$$
$$FeO = 16\%$$
$$AlO_3 = 13\%$$
$$CaO = 12\%$$
$$MgO = 8\%$$
$$TiO_2 = 7\%$$
$$other = 1\%$$

Si = silicon; O = oxygen; Fe = iron; Al = aluminum; Ca = calcium; Mg = magnesium; Ti = titanium

## Moonquakes

The Moon undergoes roughly three-thousand very minor tremors each year, most of them so small as to be unnoticeable. The most common time for moonquakes is at perigee, when the Moon is closest to the Earth and the strain on its crust from Earth's gravity pull is strongest. There has never been a serious injury or fatality from a moonquake, nor any damage that amounted to more than a minor inconvenience.

## Water

No water has been found on the Moon, although exploration teams are actively seeking pockets of ice that may exist in "cold traps" in the polar regions, where there are areas permanently shaded from sunlight.

The lunar rocks themselves appear to be totally lacking in hydrated compounds. To this day, no lunar rocks have been found to contain water in any form. In contrast, terrestrial rocks and even certain types of meteorites—carbonaceous chondrites, most notably—contain water chemically linked to the other elements in the rock, in the form of hydrates. The fact that no hydrates have been found in lunar rocks may indicate that water has never existed on the Moon.

In consequence, Moonbase must manufacture its own water or import water from elsewhere.

Although no water exists in the lunar rocks, the regolith does contain a small but significant amount of hydrogen. The solar wind, which is essentially a constant outflowing of hydrogen plasma from the Sun, impacts on the lunar surface. While much of the hydrogen is boiled away during the high temperatures of the lunar day, an average of 50 to 200 parts per million of hydrogen remains imbedded in the loosely grained regolith. This is equivalent to 0.04 percent to 0.18 percent water (when mixed with oxygen), by weight, far too little to provide the water Moonbase needs.

Moonbase imports hydrogen from Earth. It is combined with oxygen (which is abundant in lunar rocks) to make water. It may be possible in the relatively near future to make Moonbase self-sufficient in water, especially if sites richer in hydrogen than the average regolith are found, or if deposits of hydrated rocks (possibly the remains of a hydrate-rich meteorite) are located.

### Other Volatiles

Two additional elements that are important for life support, yet lacking on the Moon, are carbon and nitrogen. Both are imported regularly from Earth, in various forms. As noted above, lunar rock is also deficient in sodium, potassium, and generally in metals heavier than iron.

Plans are being developed to seek water and other necessary volatiles from asteroids whose orbits bring them relatively close to the Earth–Moon system. Other possible sources of water and volatiles include Mars, the two Martian moons, and any of several comets. (For further discussion of these possibilities, see the "Hub of the Solar System" chapter, p. 120.)

### Solar Energy

Because the Moon has no air to absorb sunlight, about twice the amount of solar energy reaches the lunar surface as reaches the surface of Earth. Without clouds to block sunlight during the 350-hour-long day, the Moon is an ideal place for utilizing solar energy.

Most of Moonbase's electrical power is generated by solarvoltaic cells. Made of lunar silicon, these simple devices convert sunlight directly into electricity. Unfiltered sunlight is also used directly in solar furnaces, where mirrors concentrate the light of the Sun to produce temperatures of many thousands of degrees—without burning an ounce of fuel, and without a gram of pollution.

### Radiation

As noted in earlier sections, the lunar surface is

exposed to dangerous levels of hard radiation from the Sun and cosmic sources. All surface structures and vehicles are shielded against normal radiation fluxes, but during a solar storm radiation levels can rapidly increase to lethal levels despite such shielding. Radiation shelters will protect you even against the fiercest solar storms; whenever a radiation alert is issued, all personnel on the surface must go to the nearest radiation shelter immediately and remain there until notified that it is safe to emerge.

All of Moonbase itself, including the Main Plaza, is protected by many meters of lunar soil against all radiation flux.

Radiation exposure is measured in *rads*, which is defined as the energy released by radiation when it is absorbed by living tissue. Thus the rad is a measure of the radiation dose actually absorbed by human tissue. One rad equals 100 ergs per gram (less than one ten thousandth of a calorie per ounce). This is an extremely small amount of energy, but even a small amount may have serious biological consequences.

In the temperate latitudes of Earth at sea level, the mean radiation dose coming in from space is from 0.20 to 0.40 rads per year. Most of this is absorbed by the atmosphere before it reaches the surface. On the Moon's surface, the dose is from 13 to 25 rads per year. A solar flare can dramatically increase that amount, however. Solar flares often drench the Moon with more than 1,000 rads over a period of a few hours to a day or more.

On Earth the average person is subjected to a

total of .2 of a rad per year (200 millirads), from the following sources:

  Natural radioactivity in bones: 34 mr/yr
  Cosmic radiation: 30 mr/yr
  Background radiation (rocks, buildings,
    etc): 48 mr/yr
  Medical X rays: 75 mr/yr
  Other manmade sources: 12 mr/yr

As noted above, the actual background radiation in Moonbase is somewhat lower than 200 mr/yr. Workers on the lunar surface, however, are exposed to a higher radiation environment. Their radiation exposure levels are constantly monitored by the Department of Health and Safety, and no surface worker is allowed to exceed 100 millirads per week, which is three times lower than the allowable dose rate for nuclear power workers on Earth.

### 2. Sample Employment Agreement

You are required to sign this Employment Agreement as a condition of your employment at Moonbase.

*Read your agreement carefully.*

If you have any questions about specific clauses or about your responsibilities under the agreement, contact a Human Resources counselor.

## MOONBASE INC. EMPLOYMENT AGREEMENT

This agreement, made and entered into this _____day of _____, 20 ____, by and between Moonbase Inc., a lunar corporation, hereinafter referred to as "Moonbase," and _____, a resident of the State of _____, County of _____, in the Nation of _____, hereinafter referred to as "Employee,"

The parties, for and in consideration of the mutual and reciprocal covenants and agreements hereinafter contained, do contract and agree as follows, to wit:

1. *Purpose.* The purpose of this Agreement is to define the relationship between Moonbase and the Employee. Moonbase hereby employs Employee, and Employee hereby accepts employment by Moonbase upon the terms and conditions herein contained. The Employee shall be required to serve his term of employment at Moonbase's main center or at another location on the Moon, at the discretion of Moonbase management officers.

2. *Term.* The term of this agreement shall commence on the _____ day of _____, 20 ____, and shall continue for a minimum of one (1) year, unless earlier terminated as provided herein.

3. *Services.* The Employee shall exert his or her best efforts and devote his or her working time and attention to the the tasks specified in the Employee's job description, as assigned to the Employee by his or her supervisor(s). The Employee shall be responsible for carrying out all authorized work-related activities, subject to the direction, approval, and control of said supervisor(s).

4. *Compensation.* As compensation for the services to be rendered by the Employee, Moonbase shall pay the Employee a fee at the annual rate of _____ U.S. Dollars (U.S. $ _____ ) per year, payable monthly at the rate of _____ U.S. Dollars (U.S. $ _____ ) per monthly payment.

In addition, Employee will receive _____shares of common stock in Moonbase Inc. This stock may not be sold until Employee terminates his or her employment agreement with Moonbase, and then it shall be sold to Moonbase Inc. at the current market value at the time of transaction. Employee is free to purchase additional shares of Moonbase Inc., and may sell them at any time to any person or entity.

## MOONBASE INC. EMPLOYMENT AGREEMENT

5. *Medical, Disability, and Life Insurance.* Moonbase agrees to provide basic hospital and medical and psychotherapeutical services to Employee, including the cost of pharmaceuticals and rehabilitative therapy, should Employee become sick or injured during the term of this Agreement. Moonbase further agrees to provide Employee with life insurance in the amount of _____ U.S. Dollars (U.S. $ _____ ) and disability insurance not to exceed _____ U.S. Dollars (U.S. $ _____ ) per month.

6. *Assumption of Risk.* Moonbase and Employee hereby covenant and agree that Employee's duties hereunder entail substantial risk to Employee's life and health. Accordingly, Employee, his or her heirs, assigns, and successors in interest, hereby agree to hold Moonbase harmless from such death or injury arising from any cause other than the wanton conduct or gross negligence of Moonbase.

7. *Expenses.* The Employee shall also be entitled to reimbursement for all reasonable expenses necessarily incurred by him or her in the performance of his or her duties upon presentation of a voucher indicating the amount and the business purposes. The Employee's reimbursement shall include, but not be limited to, a nonaccountable water allowance of _____U.S. Dollars (U.S. $ __ ) per month, and reasonable and necessary expenses incurred in obtaining special equipment and/or personalized protective apparel.

8. *Termination.* In the event that the Employee shall be prevented from rendering services or performing his or her duties hereunder by reason of illness, incapacity, or injury for a period of sixty (60) consecutive days arising during the term of this Agreement then and in such event Moonbase may terminate this Agreement upon twenty (20) days written notice to the Employee. Further, Employee may be terminated for cause as defined elsewhere.

9. *Payment Upon Termination.* If the Employee dies during the term of this Agreement, or if this Agreement is terminated under paragraph 8 because of the Employee's disability, then in any of the foregoing events, the Employee or his or her estate shall be paid, as additional compensation hereunder, within forty-five (45) days after such termination, an amount equal to two (2) months' compensation or the balance due under this Contract, whichever is less.

## MOONBASE INC. EMPLOYMENT AGREEMENT

10. *Indemnity.* Moonbase shall indemnify the Employee and hold him or her harmless for any acts or decisions made by him or her in good faith while performing services for Moonbase and will use its best efforts to obtain coverage for him or her under any insurance policy now in force or hereinafter obtained during the term of this Agreement against lawsuits. Moonbase will pay all expenses including attorneys' fees actually and necessarily incurred by the Employee in connection with the defense of such act, suit, or proceeding and in connection with any appeal thereon including the cost of court settlements.

Such indemnity shall not apply, however, in cases where a legally constituted court of law finds the Employee guilty of gross misconduct, carelessness, or illegal activity, nor where the Employee has deliberately failed to carry out his or her specified exercise regime, nor where the Employee has failed to take proper action upon receiving a radiation alert warning.

11. *Termination for Cause.* If Employee shall fail to perform his or her duties, diligently, competently, and to the best of his or her ability in accordance with this Agreement for reasons other than serious physical disability or other incapacity. Moonbase may, upon written notice, terminate his or her employment. In such event, the additional payment under paragraph 9 hereof shall not be payable.

Failure to adhere to the mandatory exercise regime shall be considered cause for termination. Failure to take proper action upon receiving a radiation alert warning shall also be considered cause for termination.

12. *Production Bonus.* Should the Employee's Division or Group exceed its planned production goals during the first or any subsequent twelve (12) months of this Agreement, then in such event the Employee shall be entitled to a bonus of between _____ percent ( ___ %) and _____ percent ( ___ %) of Employee's base salary, payable at the end of such period. Actual bonus percentage will be determined by Employee's direct supervisor, subject to approval of Division or Group director. Employee has the right to appeal any dispute over bonus terms or conditions to Division or Group director.

## MOONBASE INC. EMPLOYMENT AGREEMENT

13. *Vacation.* Employee shall be entitled to _____ ( ___ ) weeks of vacation with pay plus an additional _____ ( ___ ) days with pay for attendance at professional meetings or teleconferences during each calendar year, such vacation to be taken by the Employee at such time or times as shall be approved by Employee's direct supervisor. In addition, Employee shall be entitled to such holidays as Moonbase may approve. Unused holidays and vacation may be carried from one year to another, providing that no more than the paid time from three (3) years of employment is accumulated.

Moonbase will pay the transportation costs incurred in beginning and ending the Employee's employment.

14. *Disclosure.* Employee may not, during or after the term of this Agreement, disclose any information relating to Moonbase, its officers, employees, customers, manufacturing techniques, or business or trade information, including information regarding the affairs or operations of Moonbase, without obtaining the prior written consent of Moonbase.

15. *Venue.* In any action at law or in equity, or in any administrative proceeding, arising out of any of the terms, conditions, or covenants contained in this Agreement, the parties agree that venue for such proceeding shall lie exclusively with the court of the Legal Division of the International Astronautical Authority, or, in the case of U.S. citizens, with the Federal District Court for the 12th Circuit (Extraterrestrial District).

16. *Waiver.* The waiver by either party of a breach or violation of any provision of this Agreement shall not operate as, or be construed to be a waiver of any subsequent breach hereof.

17. *Notices.* Any and all notices required or permitted under this Agreement will be sufficient if furnished in writing, sent by telemail, and registered with the Postal Service of the nation in which the Employee was last known to reside, to his or her last known residence in the case of Employee, or to the principal office of Moonbase in the case of Moonbase.

18. *Authority.* The provisions of this Agreement required to be approved by the board of directors of Moonbase have been so approved and authorized.

# MOONBASE INC. EMPLOYMENT AGREEMENT

19. *Governing Law.* The Agreement shall be interpreted, construed, and governed according to the laws of the International Convention for the Rendering of Personal Services in Space (ICRPSS).

20. *Paragraph Headings.* The paragraph headings contained in this Agreement are for convenience only and shall in no manner be construed as part of this Agreement.

21. *Counterparts.* This Agreement is executed in multiple counterparts, including counterparts stored in electronic and/or optical computer data systems, each of which shall be deemed an original and together shall construe one and the same agreement, with one counterpart being delivered to each party thereto.

22. *Time Units.* All time units referred to in this Agreement, such as but not limited to "day," "month," and "year," are terrestrial units.

IN WITNESS WHEREOF, Moonbase has caused this Agreement to be executed by its duly authorized officers and its seal to be hereunto affixed, and Employee has hereunder set his or her hand and seal, on this _____ day of _____, 20 ____.

EMPLOYER:
MOONBASE, INC.

By: _____
Title: _____

Attest:

By: _____
Title: _____

EMPLOYEE

_____          _____

**TLW12G**
**120535**

**Acknowledgments** The "lunar underground" already exists; this book is one of its products. In many locations around the United States, farsighted men and women are at work today laying the foundations for our return to the Moon and the creation of permanent habitats there.

This book began as a conversation among Hu Davis, Bill Stump, Pat Rawlings, and me as we drove through a humid Texas noontime toward a restaurant for lunch. Hu was the head of Eagle Engineering Corporation, a company he founded after retiring from NASA in 1979. Eagle is one of the first companies in the exciting new field of space industries. The idea of mining lunar oxygen, the very name Lunox, came from the men of Eagle Engineering.

Bill and Pat were Eagle employees, and still are. Hu has "retired" once again; he is no longer active with Eagle, but has a plethora of research interests cooking, some of them with the University of Texas.

They suggested doing a book about our inevitable return to the Moon. The idea was especially appealing to me because it would give me a chance to work with Pat, probably the best of the new young artists who are literally showing us what the future can be like.

Many other people contributed important ideas and information to this book. I cannot possibly name all of them; the list would outweigh the book itself. Many of them are men and women I have never met, but whose writings and researches have helped to pave our way back to the Moon. I thank them, each and every one of them. We all should thank them.

My special gratitude, however, goes to:

Hubert P. Davis, who not only helped to inspire this book, but took the time to read the draft manuscript carefully and make a vast number of insightful and very helpful suggestions.

Pat Rawlings, whose work adorns these pages, and whose care and talent helped to create the Moonbase you have just seen and read about.

Bill Stump, who provided key ideas about the construction of Moonbase, and who was always on hand to dig up the precise fact that I needed, when I needed it.

Wendell W. Mendell, Michael B. Duke, Barney Roberts, and their colleagues at NASA Johnson Space Center. They were extremely generous with their time and patient with my questions.

Neil P. Ruzic, founder and publisher of *Industrial Research* magazine and author of *Where the Winds Sleep* (Doubleday, 1970), in which many of the ideas concerning lunar manufacturing originated, including the concept of Glassteel.

Hal Clement, the well-known science fiction writer, who generously permitted me to use the idea of First Footprints, which originally appeared in his 1974 story, "Mistaken for Granted."

Timothy G. Whalen, one of Florida's brightest young lawyers, who helped me through the legal mine fields of writing the Moonbase employment contract.

Dr. David Menke, professor of astronomy and director of the Copernican Space Science Center, at Central Connecticut State University, who supplied me with crucial information about orbital mechanics and kindly checked the manuscript for accuracy.

Andy Hoffman, of United Technologies Corporation's Hamilton Standard Division, who taught me what I needed to know about the design and construction of space suits. His "nonobtainium," the nonexistent (to date) material for the ultimate space suit has become "Lunathane" in this book. Thanks also to Diane Putnam of Hamilton Standard for her help in organizing my meeting with Mr. Hoffman and his colleagues.

As I scan this list I realize that each of us has a reasonably good chance of making it to the Moon one day. When we get there, the first drink is on me!

*Ben Bova*
*West Hartford, CT*

# Index

**About the Author**   Ben Bova is the author of more than 70 futuristic novels and nonfiction books about space, science and high technology. He is the president of the National Space Society, and has been engaged in America's space program since the *Vanguard* project, several years before the creation of NASA. A prominent commentator on TV and radio, he regularly lectures to audiences ranging from college students to corporate executives. He has won the Science Fiction Achievement Award (the Hugo) six times.